Dark Associations

The Secret Life of the Conservative Party

'To understand the Tory tree, start at its roots...'

Five extraordinary years of a local Conservative Association and what it tells us about the state of the Conservative Party and our democracy.

A tale of suicide and attempted suicide, child abuse and alleged prior knowledge thereof, blackmail allegations and the arrest of hard-working volunteers, bullying, corruption, cover-ups, drunken racist violence, theft, politically directed police investigations, moral decay and fraud. All of it true, as told by the man at the centre of the maelstrom.

If you're aghast at just how dysfunctional the Conservative Party has become nationally, and how that has destroyed trust in British politics, then read about the equally dysfunctional roots of the Tory tree: it's local associations.

Events at South Tees Conservative Association, in the heart of the government's Tees Valley 'Levelling Up' test-ground, as told by its former Chairman, will tell you all you need to know about the nature of the modern Conservative Party.

CONTENTS

Foreword

A Word on Motive

Chapter 1 - 'I Wouldn't Rule it Out'

Chapter 2 - Huntcliff

Chapter 3 - Blackmail?

Chapter 4 - Blackmail 2: The Minister, Volunteer, Arrest & Suicide Attempts

Chapter 5 - The Police and *Crime* Commissioner

Chapter 6 - Ministerial Affairs or 'Falling Madly in Lust'

Chapter 7 - Drunken, Racist Violence

Chapter 8 - Boris, Ben, Buffoonery and Brexit

Chapter 9 - Dangerous Cosplay

Chapter 10 - Not a Leg to Stand On

Chapter 11 - Imran Khan

Chapter 12 - CCHQ & the Party

Chapter 13 - Hubris! The Conservative Plan to Conquer North-East England

Chapter 14 - Councillors are Revolting

Chapter 15 - General Mayhem

Chapter 16 - Dark Associations - The Future

Chapter 17 - Conclusion - The Bitter End?

Epilogue - Mugged Off

Foreword
There are many good, honest, decent people in the Conservative Party, both locally and nationally, and to those individuals I apologise for the details I feel compelled to reveal in this book.

Some whom I know personally may feel a sense of betrayal at my actions in writing this book and that, in particular, causes me considerable regret. However, I believe the contents of this book, detailing failings in the Conservative Party and in our political system generally, are of genuine public interest to the people and voters of both the North East of England and the country at large. I have only revealed identities where absolutely necessary and not broken any personal confidences unless absolutely essential in detailing events which are undoubtedly of public interest.

If this book, even in some small way, causes the Conservative Party to make changes and improve its behaviour across a whole range of issues, then it will have served its purpose. In doing so it may also allow centre-right voters such as myself to have more confidence in supporting the party in future, as there is currently no alternative political home for those of us with such views.

If however, as I fear, the Conservative Party is beyond redemption then I hope this book may contribute towards a crushing defeat at the next general election, so that something more positive may grow up in its place on the centre-right of British politics.

Meanwhile, to the reader, I hope you find this book an illuminating, informative and, not least, entertaining read.

Lee R Holmes
Former Chairman South Tees Conservatives
April 2024

A Word on Motive - Are You a Cat or a Dog Person?

Both wonderful creatures, I'm sure you'd agree, and both with their own particular attributes.

Dogs are great companions; loyal, steadfast, funny, great to keep you company on a cold winter's night by the fire or for long walks in the countryside. Always by your side, but perhaps a little too needy for some. Almost like having children, in terms of their demands on your time and freedom.

Cats, by comparison, are such wonderful free-spirits; independent, characterful, mysterious, incredible natural acrobats and also great comedians in that extra funny way, when a thoroughly graceful and dignified creature suddenly does something downright goofy. On the downside, they can be demanding and haughty, and most cat 'owners' suspect that if they died suddenly, the cat would sooner eat them rather than starve.

As someone once said, having dogs in the house is a bit like having toddlers, whereas 'owning' cats is a bit like having stroppy teenagers.

I believe that in the Conservative Party most members belong to the dog tendency: the desire to train and control something, to demand and receive utter loyalty from their companion, certainly has a 'conservative' feel.

Of course, another crucial difference between cats and dogs is in the way these wonderful animals react to mistreatment:

Mistreat a dog and it generally slinks away with its tail between its legs to brood on why it is such a miserable creature, and why it thoroughly deserves its mistreatment at the hands of its lord and master.

Mistreat a cat, on the other hand, and it will slink away and plot its revenge.

For the record, I am very much a cat person. But the truths I am about to tell are no less true for all that.

Chapter 1 - "I Wouldn't Rule it Out"

The early evening gloom was descending over Skelton-in-Cleveland, a former mining village wedged scenically between moors and sea in this remote part of the historic North Riding of Yorkshire.

A traditionally staunch Labour supporting area, rooted in its hard-working, iron-stone mining origins, the whole of rural Cleveland was now questioning its loyalties. Years of being taken for granted by Labour politicians, added to the more recent effects of Brexit and Jeremy Corbyn's Labour leadership, had left local voters open to persuasion. This area was known as the 'Land of Iron' but local opinions were becoming far more malleable.

The mood of the Conservative Party activists crammed into a volunteer's car was far from gloomy however. It was November 2019, early in the general election campaign, and the reception on the doorstep was overwhelmingly positive.

Voters, it turned out, did want to "Get Brexit Done", generally liked Boris Johnson and vehemently disliked Labour Leader Jeremy Corbyn. This animosity was most pronounced among lifetime Labour voters, of whom there were many in this part of Cleveland, and they were key to our hopes for success.

As acting Chairman of South Tees Conservative Association (strictly we were a Federation, but more on this later) I had recently been thrust into the role following the suspension by the party of my predecessor as Chairman (more on this later also.)

As a relative newcomer to the association I was largely unscathed by the long-running feuds and personality clashes that gave STCA a somewhat dubious reputation in the region. I was a 'clean-skin' in the parlance of the security services, though I had no intention of blowing anybody up. Most of the time.

Nevertheless, since joining the party locally the previous year I had 'enjoyed' a baptism of fire, especially after being elected as 'Deputy Chairman Political' in April 2019, and events had already taken on a sinister and disturbing nature (much more on this later.)

As such, the events of recent months often came up in conversation among our activists and today was no different. Opinions were often strongly held and personality clashes deeply rooted. Despite the positive political outlook in the election campaign, too often certain activists were keen to keep these differences, not to say vendettas, on the boil.

In turn, my job was to try to keep a lid on things and keep things positive. As I tried time and again to mollify competing agendas and refocus us on the job at hand in the election, I would have to respond to the barbed comments made, and in turn would often try humour to deflect and distract.

"Yes, it has been a difficult few months," I interjected, trying to change the subject, as one of the usual suspects raised our local troubles yet again, "but the show is still on the road and things are looking positive, despite our troubles."

I paused and took the psychological temperature of the car. Everybody seemed to agree, though in some cases grudgingly. Encouraged, I continued.

"The only thing we haven't had this year is a murder." I added, venturing a little humour.

"But I wouldn't rule it out."

Chapter 2 - Huntcliff

The small seaside town of Saltburn-by-the-Sea is a purpose-built, late 19th century confection of white brick terraces sat gleaming atop grassy cliffs. Its creator, Victorian industrialist Henry Pease, was an advocate of temperance and wanted his new town to be a beacon of abstinence and wholesome living. However, its original lack of public houses had long since been corrected and now it was a slightly bohemian affair of micro-pubs, trendy wine bars and arts and crafts shops.

As such I can heartily recommend a visit, even if it has no actual connection to its striking, and shall we say occasionally 'distasteful', namesake the 2023 Amazon Originals film 'Saltburn'. Henry Pease would no doubt be spinning in his grave if Amazon Prime subscriptions were available in the afterlife.

Held since 2017 by local Conservative MP Simon Clarke, as part of his marginal Middlesbrough South and East Cleveland constituency, Saltburn itself was a hotbed of left-wing Momentum activism in the local Labour Party. This was battleground territory, where left and right fought it out from their respective bases of town centre flats and terraces, to the Tory-leaning Victorian villas and 1930s semis on the outskirts of town.

Almost as if by way of deliberate contrast to this bright and airy town, Huntcliff sits dark and brooding facing Saltburn across the valley of Skelton Beck, the waters of which are often stained a sinister red by the iron deposits which gave birth to the historic mining industry in the region. Huntcliff is a broad stand of clifftop and arable farmland which, for all its barren northern beauty, has a dark and mysterious past, and also now an unfortunate present, as a suicide blackspot for despairing locals.

The long and dark history of Huntcliff is dominated by the macabre fate that befell the ancient Roman watchtower that once stood on its commanding heights, offering views far out into the North Sea and into the distance along what is now the County Durham coast.

Excavated early in the 20th century, the tower remains (remains being an apt term as most of the building had been lost over the centuries to coastal erosion) showed a once strong redoubt: a rectangular tower of considerable height surrounded by a ditch, wall and other defensive earthworks. Built in the dog-days of the Roman Empire's presence in Britannia, its purpose was to watch out for the raiders who came increasingly by sea from the north and east, to pillage the remaining wealth of the empire.

The last such raid to be witnessed by this sentinel claimed the watchtower itself among its victims.

Some dark night, lost in the centuries of time since passed, visitors had come calling to Huntcliff and its stone watchtower, and unlike modern day-trippers to Saltburn, their intentions were far from benign.

Archeological excavations showed signs of battle and burning, and most macabre of all, the still existing well-shaft gave up the skeletons of 13 victims: men, women and children.

Quite how they died, and quite why they were despatched into the dark of the well will never be known, but the story casts a suitably grim aura over the place.

In modern times, Huntcliff has gained an equally dark and unwelcome reputation as a favoured place of suicide for local people, sometimes claiming up to a dozen victims a year. The grassy banks of its upper third give way to sheer cliffs with a fatal drop onto rocks two hundred feet below. Such is the fate of anyone despairing, or unwary, enough to venture from the Cleveland Way footpath that passes close to its edge.

Tragically, it was here one late September night in 2019 that local Conservative Party activist Jade Smith chose to end her young life. The inquest into Jade's death recorded a verdict of suicide, which I am sure is correct. But what drove her to take her own life is another matter. And what role did the Conservative Party and its attitude to its volunteers, and young people in particular, play in her death?

Jade *was*, to an extent, a troubled individual, with some drug and alcohol issues in her past, and her body was found to contain high alcohol levels during her autopsy. She had been estranged from her family for several years over allegations of physical abuse, and was by some accounts struggling with the demands of her work as a carer for young adults. However, recent events in the local party, added to her previous allegations of bullying and abuse, cannot have helped her mental state when she took that fateful decision in autumn 2019.

Only 21 when she died, Jade had a brief, sparkling, but troubled career in the Conservative Party and as a minor media star, ever since her appearance a few years before on the BBC's 'Mighty Redcar' documentary series. More recently she had gained light-hearted notoriety in the press for her "I Love Boris Johnson" tattoo, received on a boozy night out with friends in Crete.

I always found Jade to be very pleasant in person and it seems she hid her troubles well. She was passionate about the causes that interested her, including her home town of Redcar, young people, and the Conservative Party. For a young person generally, but especially in the North East of England, exhibiting strong support for the Conservative Party can't have been easy, but Jade seemed feisty and committed enough to endure the mickey-taking and occasional unpleasantness from opponents.

The relationship between Jade and the Conservative Party, was however, something of a love-hate affair, and Jade had in the past fallen out with the party and left it for Ukip, only to return later as Ukip imploded..

Jade had alleged bullying in her first stint in the party, claiming that senior figures in the local association had treated her badly, and that this added to the regular abuse she received as a young Conservative from political opponents. Being a young and fervent Tory in a traditional Labour heartland is undoubtedly difficult, and it's also fair to say Jade had a personality just as big and strident as some others in the local association, which made clashes clearly quite common in the local party.

As the alleged bullying was before the time of my involvement with South Tees Conservatives I'm in no position to pass judgement on the allegations, though it would be fair to say that Jade felt her complaints had not been dealt with appropriately by the party at the time. The effects on her mental health had clearly been very detrimental as she openly, and bravely, spoke about.

Against that background, Jade had also made some very serious allegations more recently, whilst I was South Tees Deputy Chairman (Political) and I had been asked to look into them by other local party members.

My enquiries turned up a tale of child abuse, police investigations, alleged confessions to that child abuse, alleged prior knowledge within the party of those confessions and the police investigations, covertly recorded phone calls and party cover-ups. For several years now I have been unable to detail the allegations concerned for legal reasons. Now, however, I am at liberty to divulge what is a troubling episode in the local party, and with broader implications for the party at large.

As Jade is no longer able to speak up for herself, I will do my best to speak for her, whilst also trying to be fair to others caught up in the events.

Conservative councillor David Smith was also a troubled character.

Also a young volunteer in the party, though too old for the Young Conservatives, like Jade he had been active in the 'Vote Leave' campaign in the North East of England during their victorious EU referendum campaign in June 2016. That campaign was chaired and headed up by Steve Turner, a one time UKIP councillor on Redcar & Cleveland Council, since defected to the Conservative Party, some time office manager of Simon Clarke MP, and latterly the Conservative Police and Crime Commissioner for Cleveland. Much more on him later.

According to Jade, David Smith had on occasion turned up to Vote Leave campaign events high on drugs, and been sent home for such. Jacob Young MP had also been an active campaigner for Vote Leave in 2016 though I have no idea if their paths crossed during that campaign, or if he was aware of Smith's alleged drug use or other misbehaviour. I do know that Jacob was extremely dismissive of David Smith from comments he made in my presence in June of 2019. Harshly so, I felt at the time, though subsequent events may put Jacob's attitude in context.

For David Smith was easily dismissed: an odd looking character, with thinning mullet-length hair, bespectacled, overweight and usually unshaven. I placed him in his late 20s to early 30s when I first chanced across him, though he arguably looked older.

He was openly gay, nothing wrong with that of course, so am I and so are a surprising number of local Tory MPs, including Jacob Young, Matt Vickers and Peter Gibson.

Given this, I occasionally joked, quietly, that Simon Clarke, avowedly straight (more on that later) was our 'token heterosexual' MP. By early 2022 even Dehenna Davidson, Bishop Auckland MP had come out as bi-sexual (whilst somewhat oddly divorcing her first husband to shack up with another *man*).

David Smith, once elected as a councillor for Coulby Newham, a modern, purpose-built suburb of Middlesbrough, had made a name for himself advocating for unisex toilets at Middlesbrough Town Hall, as part of his campaign to support trans rights. He was a regular at Middlesbrough's now only gay bar; a drag bar located glamorously near the bus station named 'Sapphires.' Presumably here, he was on good terms with the drag queens, who are not yet victims of some trans activists' censorious approach to a humorous take on gender dysphoria.

Having met David Smith a few times at party social and campaign events my impression was he was a (relatively) harmless eccentric, no more than that. But the local notoriety he gained from his campaigning on trans rights would come back to haunt him, and the trans and gay community, surprisingly quickly.

A taste of the problems yet to come with David emerged shortly after his election as a councillor in May 2019. Comments he had made on a football message forum had been picked up by the press and they were problematic to say the least. For both Smith and the party he represented.

'Fly me to the Moon' is a local internet forum for fans of the beloved local football team, Middlesbrough FC, or simply 'the Boro' to the local faithful (myself included.) In an example of how the internet and social media are now pretty much eternal, comments Smith had made back in 2014 came back to haunt him just over a month after his election.

Posting as 'Smoggy89' Smith had commented on the forum that a 'heinous benefit system' had led to 'rotten pond life families that should be sterilised and washed' So not exactly opinions that the modern Conservative Party wanted to be associated with. Rather more the epitome of the 'nasty party' the then Tory leader Theresa

May had famously denounced the Conservatives as being at risk of becoming.

On being challenged on these views on the forum at the time, Smith had backtracked somewhat, clarifying that he wasn't talking about *all* benefit claimants, that there were many deserving cases, but that there was a large portion of claimants that take the 'absolute Pi$$'.

'Yet they continue to breed.' He continued. 'Rabbits, the lot of them.'

So the second dose of backtracking had rather undone the mollifying effect of the first dose of backtracking!

Needless to say, when the local paper the Gazette and its online site Teesside Live, broke the story in June 2019 Smith's apologies were profuse. He apologised for the comments 'unreservedly' though went on to reassert that welfare dependency was morally wrong and that he was proud Conservative welfare reforms had drastically cut unemployment.

The local Labour party naturally made hay with such comments, claiming they reflected a wider contempt in the Tory Party and helped expose failings in the very policies Smith championed.

The whole episode, perhaps, goes some way to explain why rumour had it that Smith had originally approached Labour to stand for them in the local elections, but that he had been rejected. 'Barge Poles' and an aversion to touching him with them had apparently been mentioned. In an area like Teesside it is always easier for Labour to find candidates than for the Tories, and as a result the local Tories are a little less choosy in candidate selection than they should be.

The party *does* impose rules on candidate choice, having in place a two stage process: firstly 'approvals' to check that potential candidates are of good standing and unlikely to cause the party embarrassment, followed by 'selection' where potential candidates are allocated to particular wards. I was not involved in any part of that process for the 2019 local elections, other than as a candidate myself, so I have no inside knowledge as to what transpired at the time. However, it was later alleged that Smith had not been through that process at all, but had been 'parachuted' into Coulby Newham at a very late stage.

That may explain why Smith's earlier comments on social media had not come to light, though the social media searches recommended by the party nationally seemed scant, if present at all, in South Tees. Another of our 2019 local election candidates, Cllr Lee Holmes of Skelton (not me! More on this weird coincidence later) had fallen foul of previous facebook comments dating back several years, so the risk was well proven.

The apparent lack of a formal vetting and approvals process was to come back to haunt the party shortly, and would form the basis of Jade Smith's explosive allegations against the local party.

For later that summer, Smith was formally charged by Cleveland Police with numerous counts of sexual offences against young boys dating back several years. These included various counts of the sexual touching of a child, and would later be upgraded to alleged rape when a further victim came forward.

Jade Smith alleged to various local members, including myself, that there was prior knowledge in the party of these allegations and the police investigations, *and* an alleged confession by Smith to having sex with an underage boy, *before* he was selected to stand for the party.

Such an allegation was explosive, suggesting a complete disregard for both safeguarding and the potential reputational damage to the party. But how to prove it? Jade was going to try.

I was contacted by another local Conservative, also a member of the STCA Executive, to tell me that Jade had secretly recorded a telephone conversation with a senior party figure locally and that in the call she challenged them on David Smith and alleged prior knowledge of Smith's offending.

Jade's motives for this were numerous. Jade worked with vulnerable adults and children as a carer and support worker, and her concerns about safeguarding were genuine enough. In the past, Jade herself had been the Chairman of the local Young Conservatives group, and as the YCs take members from the age of 15 upwards there ARE genuine concerns about safeguarding of young members within the party. Her own previous allegations of bullying from more senior local members of the party whilst in that role perhaps gave her an even stronger personal interest in the issue of safeguarding younger members. Jade also volunteered with youngsters in the Brownies and her concern for safeguarding was no doubt intensified by this.

History suggests that councillors and other politicians have regularly abused their positions to access and abuse children. Cyril Smith and Greville Janner spring to mind as particularly grotesque examples. In which case, why on earth would a political party take the chance of putting such an individual in a position of trust?

On the other hand, Jade arguably had a less honourable motive in making such allegations, and that was a serious falling out with the party locally and some of its senior local members.

As mentioned, Jade had something of a love-hate relationship with the party and local officials and I suspect that feeling was mutual. Though, for all Jade's later, posthumous twitter allegations of abuse within the party I have no reason to think that she included local party officials in those allegations.

In particular Jade had a strong connection with our then Chairman Malcolm Griffiths. Whilst at times turbulent, their relationship appeared that of a surrogate grandfather-surrogate granddaughter kind of thing, given Jade was estranged from her own family. Malcolm appeared the often exasperated fatherly figure trying to keep Jade on the straight and narrow, and given Jade's volatile personality that was bound to be a tumultuous task, and lead to disagreements.

Specifically, Malcolm had stood Jade down as a party candidate in a winnable target ward in the 2019 local elections, much to her anger. The reason was that Jade had responded to an error in the production of one of her election leaflets by our campaign manager, that led to the leaflets being unusable, with a foul mouthed tirade. The decision to stand her down was probably correct, such volatility *within the party* is bad enough but if directed at the public could prove extremely damaging. But did it also give Jade a very personal attitude to David Smith being allowed to go forward as a candidate? And a personal grudge against the association?

Malcolm, for all his many flaws and ill-judged facebook posts (more on this later), is at heart, I think, a decent man. Old school, yes, but in my dealings with him (and at times they were pretty fraught) I generally found him to be a reasonable, if stubborn, individual. He was set in his ways, and with a long history in the party dating back many decades, and this often caused friction with me as a newcomer and moderniser. His subsequent expulsion from the party a couple of months later over his ill-judged facebook comments on Islam was undoubtedly deserved, but also undoubtedly left him feeling ill-rewarded for those years of service.

Malcolm had the reputation for being something of a schemer in the local party, a great survivor who had been Chairman for many years (his current tenure had been disputed, unsuccessfully, by a rival as being beyond the limit set by party rules.) Like some spider sat at the centre of a web, Malcolm would feel the vibrations of rumours emanating in the local party, playing potential rivals off against one another, and luring potential allies, servants, or victims into his clutches. Nothing unusual for a long term survivor of South Tees Conservative's notoriously fractious and volatile internal politics.

For all the allegations of racism and islamophobia that he would later face, and that would lead to his expulsion by CCHQ, in many ways Malcolm was a bit of a 'new man.' In response to the facebook comments that brought him down he would proudly recount how he had had muslim business partners on many occasions in the past and traded with the subcontinent in antiques and arts and crafts, many of which he was proud to display in his home. He also had a female life partner from Asia, reputedly (in local party legend) rescued by Malcolm from some form of modern-day slavery in a restaurant he had once visited. If true, it certainly painted the man in an admirable light.

In addition, he had been in the past very supportive of two young members of the association who came out as gay, in times when society and the party in particular was less accepting. That young couple included Peter Gibson who would subsequently go on to become Conservative MP for Darlington.

I had heard rumours that Malcolm had been dismissive of Jacob Young, now MP for Redcar and also openly gay, but that was more to do with his youth and inexperience as a teenage party candidate, rather than his sexuality. On one alleged occasion, Jacob had approached Malcolm with a view to being the party candidate for Middlesbrough South and East Cleveland, our marginal seat locally, in the snap general election called by Theresa May in 2017. Malcolm had allegedly laughed at the suggestion, though I have only gossip in support of this particular tale. It sounded believable to me, all the same.

Malcolm and myself had a difficult relationship at times, as he often seemed to want to block the modernisation changes I was eager to introduce as DCP, and had an interesting approach to party rules (often seeming to make them up as he went along) I never sensed that my own sexuality was in any way a factor in this, however.

Malcolm, like many people of his generation was a product of his upbringing and that change from the strictly regimented and moralistic 1940s and 1950s to the far more permissive 'swinging '60s' As such his attitude to gays was pretty liberal, especially for a Conservative.

Malcolm was also a great teller of anecdotes, often repeatedly, and one of his favourites was how he had once been arrested by the local constabulary based on the suspicion caused by his lodging with another single man, at a time before the 1967 reforms that decriminalised homosexuality. He had even been kept in a cell overnight, and the coppers' suspicions were only allayed by his then girlfriend turning up with cigarettes for him the next morning. Such experiences of a less accepting time no doubt coloured his own attitudes and *may* have led him to take a too accepting attitude to David Smith and his much publicised out-there views on gender, trans-issues and sexuality.

Regardless of Jade's motives for seeking to uncover what was known in the party of Smith's past behaviour, the potential damage it might cause was immense. When I was informed of Jade's telephone recording, I was immediately back in fire-fighting mode, which, in my experience, seems to be the default setting for a DCP at South Tees Conservatives.

Here was an alleged scandal that could have caused serious reputational damage to the party, both locally and nationally, at a time of great political uncertainty. With the Brexit impasse rumbling on, disunity in the party and active rebellion and indiscipline among our MPs, the potential for yet another general election was never far from the horizon.

In addition there was the safeguarding concern that Jade's allegation raised. If true, it did create genuine concerns about how we protected young members and other vulnerable children and adults from potential predators, who always gravitate to opportunities for abuse. I decided to contact Jade, to investigate, ideally to hear the recording myself (as at that point I only had second hand accounts of what it supposedly disclosed) and also to impress upon her the legal requirement not to make this recording or the allegations it contained public.

Quite apart from the huge capacity for bad publicity for the party, at an already difficult time, there was the even more pressing matter of contempt of court and the sub-judice rules. Now that Smith had been formally charged with sexual offences and the matter was effectively before the courts, any such disclosure of allegations about past offending by Smith would itself be a criminal offence. It was essential, for Jade's own well-being as much as anything else, that she was made aware of this, and the vital importance of it impressed upon her.

The now seemingly ubiquitous facebook messenger was a favoured means of communication among local Conservative members and I had already messaged Jade on the platform previously, so chose to contact her by those means.

In her reply, Jade seemed genuinely angry that she felt her confidence on this matter had been breached by the few members who she had informed of her allegations, all of whom, like herself, had issues with the association. Others who had been rivals of Malcolm for the Chairmanship, who had themselves also been stood down by Malcolm from winnable wards for debatable reasons, or with a belief that Malcolm had let them down in other matters, did have reasons to see the association, and Malcolm's leadership of it especially, brought down by such allegations.

At that stage, I wasn't one of them. For all Malcolm was a block to the progress I wished to bring to STCA, I had determined to try to work with him, or if necessary *around him,* to do so. As such I was something of an honest broker in the affair with no personal skin in the game. My aims were to make sure the contempt of court rules weren't broken, that negative publicity for the party was avoided, or if necessary delayed, and that Jade's concerns over safeguarding within the party were properly addressed. A complicated balancing act in the circumstances.

Jade was open to me hearing the recording when I explained my reasons for wanting to do so, and assured her that I took her concerns about safeguarding seriously and was the best person locally to do something about it. We initially agreed to meet in her native Redcar, with me offering to buy her a coffee in a quiet cafe somewhere. A date was set and I impressed upon Jade the necessity not to go public with what she was alleging. Fortunately, she was already well aware of the contempt rules and was, in addition, concerned about her own potential liability for making a secret recording without the other party's knowledge or consent.

However, within a couple of days another local party and Executive Council member contacted me to say that she was meeting Jade at home to listen to the recording and decide what to do about it. This member also had reasons to dislike Malcolm's leadership of the association and in combination with Jade was potentially explosive. I immediately asked to attend as well, to head off any risk of immediate disclosure and breach of the law.

The afternoon came and I travelled to Middlesbrough and the member's house, an elegant Victorian villa in a once select, but now slightly down-at-heel part of town. Over coffee the three of us sat in the front room, Jade clasping the laptop that contained the recording protectively on her lap. She explained how outraged she was at the content of the recording and the circumstances it revealed. She added that the thought of Smith abusing youngsters turned her stomach, especially when she was working with the children she volunteered with.

I assured Jade that I took the allegations very seriously and understood the need to ensure that proper safeguarding was followed at South Tees. I would proceed with her concerns on any basis she felt comfortable with, bearing in mind the legal rules we were now all constrained by. On that basis she was happy to let me listen to the recording.

I listened to the recording a couple of times on that one and only occasion and it was a reasonably clear record of the telephone call between Jade and a senior figure in the local party. In it Jade raised her concerns about David Smith and her amazement that the party had allowed someone like him, with his background, to become a Conservative councillor. Crucially, she made the allegation directly in that recording that Smith had abused an underage boy, that he had confessed to that abuse and that there was knowledge of that in the party prior to Smith being allowed to stand for the party in a winnable target ward.

My recollection is that the response to that direct accusation on the recording was non committal, the party figure neither denied nor accepted the assertion that they were aware of any such confession, but instead gave a kind of resigned grunt in response.

Now, if I had been accused of allowing a self-confessed paedophile to stand for election for the party, with all the safeguarding and reputational risk that that entailed, I would have denied it forcefully, if it were untrue. I believe most people would do so in the same circumstances and so, to me, the response was telling. If Jade's assertions were untrue, why didn't they deny them? And forcefully so.

The rest of the conversation on the recording was much as I expected. Jade was angry, and had every right to be, given the circumstances.

I am not naming the other party to the conversation Jade recorded, as without access to the recording Jade made, I would be on shaky legal ground to do so. What became of the recording, I do not know. Following Jade's death her belongings presumably ended up with friends or family, but whether they could access the laptop that held it, I also do not know.

Of the central allegation regarding Smith's selection for the party to fight a winnable ward, the other party to the recording alleged that several senior local party figures were involved in making that selection and endorsing it. Despite the fact that Smith had not been properly vetted as a candidate and, in some cases at least, in knowledge of Smith's previous admission to sexual activity with underage boys. This makes the case even more disturbing, if true.

Smith was eventually convicted of several charges of child sexual abuse, including rape, following a trial much delayed by covid restrictions in April 2022. He was sentenced to 12 years imprisonment for his crimes, and deservedly so.

Taking all the above into account I have no reason to doubt that Jade's assertion that Smith was allowed to stand for the Conservative Party while senior party figures were aware of inappropriate, and potentially criminal behaviour, was well founded. Given what we now know about Smith's offending and the circumstances of his selection Jade had every right to feel seriously aggrieved about what had transpired. But at the time, back in summer 2019, the question was, what to do about it?

At the meeting where I listened to Jade's recording I emphasised that we had to be very careful not to break the sub-judice laws and commit contempt of court. Jade agreed not to make the recording or the allegations it contained public and not to tell others about it, except if she raised a formal complaint under safeguarding procedures within the party. My knowledge of contempt laws was sketchy, and the law in places is vague, but that approach appeared to both keep us safe whilst raising legitimate concerns within the party. Jade said she had no confidence in the local or regional party structures, given her previous experiences and so would make a complaint to CCHQ directly. I said I thought that was a sensible approach, and encouraged Jade to raise her concerns and allegations with CCHQ. Jade assured me she would.

Whether Jade did this, I don't know for sure, but she was certainly not the kind of character to let such matters lie. Another local party activist, who was closely involved in the matter, is adamant that

Jade both phoned CCHQ initially with her allegations and followed up with a written complaint. In a forwarded message from Jade, she confirmed that she had spoken to CCHQ about Smith's selection by phone.

If Jade did raise these very troubling matters with CCHQ, I never heard any more about it, despite being Deputy Chairman and then Chairman of STCA. This appears to follow a pattern within the Conservative Party of covering up, or simply ignoring, safeguarding issues, and other scandals, that is apparent in numerous cases. It is the culture of the Conservative Party to do so.

Communications from CCHQ to local associations can also often be poor: there seems to be a reluctance to keep mere volunteers informed on important matters from the 'professional' (ie. paid) side of the party. Overall there is an attitude of disdain, if not contempt, for the 'voluntary' party from paid staff, despite the fact it's the volunteers who keep the party running.

CCHQ often seemed like an information 'black-hole': we fed information into the centre but rarely, if ever, seemed to get very much back, including answers to simple queries or even important complaints. If Jade did raise these matters before her tragic suicide in September 2019, what CCHQ did with them is a mystery. Nothing as far as I'm aware.

I suspect the culture within the party would be to sit on the complaint, perhaps using the court proceedings as a reason why nothing could be done, and then drop it quietly after Jade's death. Certainly, there was no contact by the party centrally with me as Chairman about these issues, or the other allegations raised by Jade in posthumous tweets detailed later in this chapter.. Such is the culture in the party, where it's deemed better to drop difficult issues rather than rock the boat. Defending the party is paramount.

Whether the prospect of Jade's complaint to CCHQ would satisfy the others locally who had an axe to grind against the association was another issue. Quickly I got wind that certain local activists were pressing for a Special General Meeting to call for a vote of no confidence in Malcolm's chairmanship of the association, citing the charges against Smith, and the fact he had ever been allowed to stand for the party. Such an approach was fraught with danger, both for the party's reputation and for the prospect of Smith getting a fair trial.

I contacted our Regional Chairman for a steer on the likely consequences of such a move. His advice was that a Special General Meeting and vote of no confidence in such circumstances would see STCA placed into 'special measures' with the party machine taking control. Added to this Malcolm had already made plain that he wouldn't resign even if he lost a vote of confidence, and under party rules it was pretty clear he would not be forced to do so. So the damage of a SGM and vote of no confidence would also prove an utterly pointless self-inflicted wound.

In a series of sharp messenger exchanges I sought to dissuade the ringleaders from taking this course of action and trying to arrange a petition to force a SGM.

'Malcolm won't resign anyway even if he loses a vote' I argued.

'Under party rules he wouldn't have to step down either' I added.

'If it does go ahead we'll likely be placed into special measures and even if we weren't, I would be unwilling to serve under a Chairman who had lost a vote of confidence, and I'd have to resign instead!"

Despite assertions that they had the signatures to force such an SGM and vote of no confidence, the attempted coup fizzled out and STCA struggled on. Whether the support had been there or not is unclear, the ringleaders had a reputation for being prone to exaggeration and, maybe it was all bluster to try to force Malcolm out. Either way, chaos had been narrowly averted, and the usual state of mere disorder restored.

For my efforts, the party avoided yet another scandal, Malcolm soldiered on and I had to continue trying to work around him to move things forward.

From some of the conspirators I was attacked as a 'weak and useless Deputy Chairman'. Such are the slings and arrows of local politics but a worse outcome had been avoided, and events would soon mean change at the top of STCA was achieved anyway, in slightly less chaotic fashion.

However, even closer events were about to take a truly tragic turn.

On the morning of October 1st 2019 I woke up in my hotel in Manchester, and started getting myself ready for a day at Conservative Party Conference at the Gmex Centre. This wonderful former railway station, consisting of a single great arch of cast iron and glass, a tremendous example of Victorian engineering at its most impressive and elegant, was jam packed with exhibitors and campaigners, each selling their own particular brand of product or ideas. Conference could be fun and frustrating in equal measure, but either way you felt you had to be there.

As I pulled on a shirt and tie my mobile phone rang and I struggled over to pick it up before it rang off.

"Hello" I answered, tugging on a shirt sleeve as I picked the phone off the desk.

"Lee, I have some terrible news," It was Jill, a fellow STCA Executive Council member, "Jade Smith, has fallen to her death at Huntcliff."

In that sudden moment of shock I wasn't sure whether I had heard correctly, and for a few seconds actually thought I had heard that *Dave* Smith had been found dead. Such were our concerns following his charging with child sex offences, that he had been on a kind of suicide watch, with the then chairman and his council colleagues taking a pastoral interest in his state of mind and personal circumstances. We all still held the concept of 'innocent unless proven guilty' dear, despite the seriousness of the charges against him.

Never for a moment would I have thought that Jade Smith would have been the victim of a lonely suicide at that eerie place on the Cleveland coast. Surely, she was too feisty a character to do such a thing? The last time I spoke to her she seemed positive and keen to get involved again.

As Jill continued, my confusion cleared and the dawning horror of what I was hearing sank in.

Jade's body had been found the previous Sunday, at the foot of Huntcliff, Jill had heard about a death at the cliff earlier, but the identity had only now been confirmed to her.

I sat down in shock and was at a loss for words, eventually expressing my horror and sadness but declining to say what we would do next before saying goodbye and hanging up. The thought of somebody so young and full of life choosing to end that life in such a cold and desolate place was too horrible to comprehend. Recent events in the local party made it all the more chilling. Of course, the cause of death couldn't be determined until an inquest verdict, but given the location and circumstances it appeared all too tragically obvious that Jade had taken her own life.

As the conference went on for the next couple of days, further revelations from Jade came to media attention in the form of tweets she had scheduled to come from her Twitter account after her apparently planned death. These must have been intended to go public during Conservative Party conference.

Her account was then swiftly shut down but several of these tweets were made public, and were taken up by both the national and international press. For they made allegations about previous bullying she had suffered in the party and of sexual abuse within the party, particularly at conference, as she recounted young party activists all too often falling prey to older, predatory men.

Beneath the obligatory photo of Jade posing with her hero Boris Johnson (and there's no suggestion Jade found him anything but an absolute gentleman) papers such as The Metro domestically, and the New York Post internationally, carried Jade's heartfelt final words.

"There's one last topic I want to talk about before I go and say my goodbye. This is the last time I'll ever have a platform to ask them to change, to beg them for young people's sake to change."

"Back in 2015/2016 I tried to kill myself several times because of the Tory party,". **"I was institutionalized due to bullying and harassment I received. I was stalked by the press, the press stood outside my college with cameras."**

"But the abuse we receive from each other and the older people in our associations is what takes it too far. We shouldn't have to put up with the bullying from each other. We shouldn't have to be worried that our friends are going to be raped at conference or at the very least sexually assaulted. We shouldn't have to put up with creepy weird old men maturating

over us or grabbing us to go and chat to their friends and try to take us home at the end of the night. There's a reason we don't feel safe at conference."

This last tweet was particularly troubling and poignant, as until that point I had felt that if only Jade had come to conference that year she would never have felt so despairing that she would have been driven to suicide. She seemed so full of life and fun that she would have been feted at conference, especially as such a committed Boris fan under his freshly installed leadership. Little did I know that previous conference trips had proved so troubling for her.

In response to Jade's posthumous allegations the Conservative Party promised a full investigation into her treatment and her allegations, publicly in the national and international media.

I have to say that as her Deputy Chairman Political at South Tees, and about a month later the acting Chairman, and as someone who encouraged her to raise her local allegations with CCHQ, I was NEVER contacted by the Conservative Party by any such promised investigation. Nor was I ever made aware, as Chairman, of any conclusions from such an investigation.

All I can conclude from that is that no such party investigation ever took place, or if it did it was so superficial and scant that I was never contacted as a potential witness, nor informed of its findings as local Chairman.

The Conservative Party talks a good game on safeguarding, especially in response to the tragic and troubling suicide of a young party activist such as Jade, but in truth as soon as the media interest had blown over it seems the party is content to do nothing, and instead to bury the allegations of abuse and bullying alongside its victims. Because the sad fact is that in the current Conservative Party the only thing that matters is cynical self-preservation, and covering the party's back at all costs. That is its culture.

After the conviction of David Smith in early 2022, when the questions about his prior behaviour and knowledge of it within the party were no longer sub-judice, I raised Jade's allegations about Smith with CCHQ. And got absolutely nowhere. I, and the allegations Jade made, were ignored. The cover-up culture in the party is alive and well.

I also raised my concerns about all the above events at South Tees (in an association next door to his own) with Prime Minister Rishi Sunak's constituency agent, by means of an attempt to bypass the cover-up culture at CCHQ. I received no response from Rishi's office either.

Of course Jade's death wasnt the first suicide of a young Conservative Party activist, it followed that of Elliott Johnson in 2015 also at the age of 21. Elliott had been a party activist in 'Conservative Future' a youth wing of the party and his experience also involved apparently destructive bullying, and attempts within the party to get him to drop complaints about it.

Given this previous suicide, Jade's own tragic death, and the further suicide attempts of Conservative activists I will detail later in this book, it is clear that the Conservative Party has a cultural problem in the way it treats its own people. Not least the abuse and bullying of those who are vulnerable. It's a fair question to ask that if it treats its own in such a way, should we be surprised at the way it treats the vulnerable in the wider community?

This itself is disturbing enough, but it is also clear from these tragic examples, and the further abuses detailed in this book, that the Conservative Party has no interest in addressing its culture, or the abuses that occur under it.

Only in covering them up.

A Troubling Postscript on Huntcliff

As a keen walker who lives in the East Cleveland town of Loftus, which lies in between the barren beauty of the North York Moors National Park and the Cleveland Way National Trail that runs along the local coastline, I'm regularly out rambling in these parts. I can highly recommend the area's cliffs, beaches and moors to anyone who loves the outdoors.

One of my regular walks takes me from home to the charming hamlet of Hummersea, a one time location of the 2016 Dad's Army film remake. This includes the cottage used as Catherine Zeta

Jones' rental in the film, that sits hunkered down upon the rugged clifftops, albeit without the crafty bit of CGI used in the film to turn the cliffs from sandstone buff to a chalky white.

From there you are faced with the choice of turning right along the coast to head up and over Boulby Cliff, the highest point on the east coast of England, and then down to the stunning fishing village and artist's colony of Staithes. Alternatively, turning left and heading a similar distance down to the characterful village of Skinningrove and on to Saltburn by the Sea, along equally stunning cliffs. The Saltburn option takes you along Huntcliff, and I must have walked that way many dozens of times.

In late summer 2023, I was returning from Saltburn along the clifftop path over Huntcliff after just such a regular walk. The day was changeable, though for the moment as I approached the site of the old Roman signal station and watch tower I was bathed in beautiful late-afternoon sunshine that seemed to illuminate the small patch of ground I was traversing to the exclusion of the surrounding gloom. The footpath ran close to the cliff edge at this point, squeezed narrowly in between that and the golden wheat fields to the landward side.

As I scanned the footpath ahead, loping along at pace, a small part of it seemed to branch off from the main path and veer towards the cliff edge. It looked little more than a rabbit run; narrow, but clearly trodden down and inexplicably headed right up to the cliff edge and disappearing into the void beyond.

At that very point I suddenly got the most extraordinary, giddy feeling that I should also veer from the footpath and run, at speed, towards the edge, along this path to nowhere. It was an eerie, unsettling sensation, and although it was easily resisted (I wasn't in any way feeling suicidal) it struck me as truly chilling, and the appearance of this little path to oblivion very odd indeed.

Being a boring, rational sort, not given to flights of fancy, I thought little more of it, though I did keep as far back from the edge as the path would allow and did mention the experience later to my partner on our usual daily catch-up phone call.

More recently, this time in late November and in the fading light of mid afternoon, I was returning home again along the Cleveland Way footpath along the same edge of Huntcliff. The going under foot was heavy, wet and slippery and as I'd already gone down onto my hands and knees once on the outward journey, my eyes were fixated on the footpath beneath my feet, trying to pick out the driest and least slippery patches.

All of a sudden, as I looked up I realised that the path had turned towards the cliff edge and I was now only about six feet from the crumbling, grassy precipice of the cliff and the abyss beyond. The path naturally runs in that direction but I was at first surprised at how suddenly I had come so close to the edge, having been so fixated upon my footing for the past several hundred yards.

A chill ran down my spine at the proximity of death, though this is nothing unusual as part of my attraction to cliff and hill walking is being close to danger: walking a fine line between life and oblivion. This, and my natural fear of heights, makes the experience of this kind of walking all the more thrilling.

However, the sudden and forceful tug I felt on the cliff-ward sleeve of my fleece was anything but normal, and like nothing I have experienced before. It was utterly uncanny and disturbing.

As stated, I'm not a person normally given to flights of fancy or a belief in the supernatural at all, and have never before experienced something so inexplicable and eerie. Though I have always claimed, at least, and maybe out of bravado, that I would love to experience something scarily supernatural that I couldn't explain. If anything I have become more of a sceptic about such matters the older, and more boring, I have become.

It may be that this sensation of a tugging on my sleeve, trying to pull me towards the edge and a certain death on the rocks below, was entirely of my own imagining. I *had* been on a long walk, I *was* tired and breathless given my rapid pace and the climb that the cliff takes towards the corner where it turns back towards Skinningrove and home. The light *was* fading on a gloomy day with dark clouds rolling in from the west and the whole ambience *was* given to such dark imaginings

However, given these two experiences I am less of a sceptic than I was.

And if anywhere has a right to be haunted, it is this bleak and lonely cliff top.

Chapter 3 - Blackmail?

(The following Chapter had been updated in Chapter 4, detailing more recent developments, but is included to give readers a full picture of events)

I have struggled with both moral and legal quandaries before committing this chapter to paper (well, in truth, an extremely aged HP netbook rather than actual paper. This is 2024 afterall)

I have hesitated to raise the issues contained within it at all, for fear of causing legal or physical harm to the individual at the centre of the events detailed, or myself for that matter. But I'm a strong believer that people have a right to know, honestly and fully, what they are voting for when they cast their ballots at elections.

With a general election due sometime in 2024, and quite possibly a lot earlier given the parlous nature of Rishi Sunak's authority in a Tory Party now seemingly possessed of a death wish, it's important that voters hear about these events before they choose who is fit to govern them and the country.

For those same legal and moral reasons I must be vague at times in this chapter, for which I apologise in advance, but this is wholly to try to protect the innocent and vulnerable, rather than the guilty.

At one point, there also remained, despite my further attempts at uncovering the truth of the allegations made to me, the vanishingly small chance that I was the victim of some elaborate, twisted hoax, and that I was repeating falsehoods. However, given subsequent events, I wholeheartedly believe the contents of this chapter to be true. Given the circumstances in which the allegations came to me and the further enquiries I have undertaken, I now have no doubt in the veracity of the tale, though I will detail the quandaries I faced in reaching that conclusion, often having to read carefully given the issues at stake.

If on the minute chance it turns out that these allegations are mistaken, I will happily retract and apologise, and it is open to the Conservative Party to issue a full denial of the alleged events in this chapter.

The central allegation in this chapter is that the Conservative Party, and a Conservative MP, and minister, who I am not currently naming for legal reasons, had a hardworking and dedicated Conservative Party activist, *who they knew to be psychologically vulnerable,* arrested by Cleveland Police. Their home was raided, phones and laptops seized, they were locked up in a police station cell and interrogated for hours, on an allegation of blackmail *in what was to all intents and purposes a political dispute.*

If true, and I have very little reason to doubt the veracity of my sources (notwithstanding the proviso above), it would follow a pattern of the Conservative Party being willing to use the police to try to silence its critics in political disputes (take Conservative Police and Crime Commissioner Steve Turner's use of his own police force to silence critics during the local elections in 2023, detailed in a following chapter)

In short, behaviour more suited to Putin's Russia than the United Kingdom.

It would also be further proof of my central assertion in this book; that the Conservative Party's culture is now utterly corrupt and immoral, willing to do virtually anything to protect and preserve its grip on power. Now so desperate and lacking in common human decency that it would have one of the most hardworking and loyal Conservative activists I have known, *who they also knew to be a vulnerable individual,* arrested and locked up in a police cell for the most petty of reasons.

Worse than this, the activist concerned was a longstanding friend of the MP in question. With friends like these…

In addition to the moral corruption this episode illustrates, it also reveals the political ineptitude now so prevalent in the Conservative Party; for who in their right mind thought that having such a hard working volunteer arrested was the right thing to do *politically*?

For the results of this action by the Conservative Party were utterly devastating for the individual concerned and raise, once again, the troubling spectre of suicide among Conservative Party activists.

As such it also raises the question of what is it about the nature of the party and its treatment of people that makes suicide a factor in a number of tragic cases concerning Conservative activists.

It also begs the question: if the Conservative Party will treat its own like this, why should anybody be surprised by its treatment of people generally?

So, on to the facts of this disturbing episode, let me take you back to the local elections in spring 2023.

Having left the party the previous year I had become something of a low-level irritant for the Conservative Party on twitter and in the local press, as I continued researching the content for this book, pulling together reams of emails, meeting notes and other material to pen this account of my experiences at South Tees Conservatives, the various scandals I had dealt with as Chairman, and what it tells us about the party.

During this time I would occasionally comment on twitter about the party's latest misadventures, both local and national, and took particular interest in the very odd (and as it turned out very foolish) decision of Conservative Police and Crime Commissioner Steve Turner to stand for the local council whilst also serving as PCC for one of the most troubled police forces in the country. Particularly odd given the cloud under which he took the PCC position and had operated since: admitted past serious criminal behaviour and other unproved allegations of misconduct (all detailed in a later chapter)

It was that public criticism that led a former acquaintance in the party to contact me with their concerns about more recent events in the local party, including allegations of bullying and threats, and about selection decisions for candidates for the local elections, including allegations of irregularities in the selection of Mr Turner.

They also detailed concerns they had about other party candidates and also evidence of serious problems in the constituency offices of our two Conservative MPs. This included evidence that Simon Clarke MP was being sued by one of his workers, who happened to be both the wife of Steve Turner, and also the Conservative Group Leader on Redcar and Cleveland Council, Councillor Andrea Turner. All of which was of public interest with elections in the offing and voters being asked to choose their local representatives, and which parties to entrust with vital local services.

The Conservative Party was naturally keen to portray itself as a united team locally, building on the popularity of Tees Valley Mayor Ben Houchen and the whole government 'Levelling Up' agenda which was starting to bear fruit in its testing ground of Teesside.

The allegation that the Conservative Group leader on the local council, which included the main site of that Levelling Up redevelopment. was actually suing the senior local Conservative MP hardly helped that image of a unified and successful Tory team. The fact that allegation was evidenced by a message from the former Cabinet Minister MP himself, apparently confirming the dire and now litigious state of affairs in his office, was all the more problematic.

This individual supplied me with information and evidence on all the above and requested a face to face meeting to discuss it all, which I was happy to agree to, both to discuss the latest issues, and to chew over old times. We met, drank some very decent coffee, and it was clear that all was not well in the local party. Selection decisions had been flawed amid rumours of rules being broken and even darker rumours of defection threats if decisions didn't go a certain way. It was clear that this individual was not happy with how things had panned out, and had made this clear to the local party and the local Tory MPs.

Crucially, they told me that they had met with one MP in particular and had threatened to refuse to sign their own nomination papers for their own election contest given how unhappy they were with other selections and the general rule breaking within the local party. They said that the MP had made a suggestion that this amounted to blackmail, but they laughed this off as the emotive spur-of-the-moment rubbish it seemed to be.

We parted on good terms and agreed to keep in touch to try to keep abreast of the dysfunctionality in the local party. Which we did by whatsapp, text message and email.

A few days later and the local elections were coming to a head, with election day about a week away. The concerns my source had about local party selections would largely be borne out by the eventual results that would see PCC Turner not just lose his council contest but contribute to his wife losing her seat in the same ward.

This followed several recounts, over several days, with the contest being the last result to be declared in all the elections held nationally, long after election day itself. This long, protracted saga drew the attention of Sam Coates, Deputy Political Editor at Sky News who reported on it at the time, rather proving the scope for this to embarrass the party.

However, about a week before polling day my source apparently had far more pressing personal concerns and at this time I received an odd text message from an unknown number.

"Is this the number of the former Conservative Chairman Lee Holmes." It mysteriously asked, identifying my contact and former colleague in the party as the texter. "If so could you reply back."

I replied that it was indeed the correct number and how could I help?

In a series of text messages the texter recounted a horrifying tale of their current circumstances and recent experiences at the hands of the Conservative Party and Cleveland Police. They stated that they had been arrested and their usual phone seized by police, hence their use of this new number, which they said was a work phone.

They claimed that four police officers of Cleveland Police CID had raided their house unannounced, in a small tight-knit rural community with all the upset that caused. They had arrested them and taken them to a police station to be held and interviewed on an allegation of blackmail that had been made against them by the Conservative Party and, seemingly, a local Conservative MP. They were now on bail, still without their usual phone, and under restrictions as to their movements.

It concerned me whether they were breaching those conditions even by contacting me, but it was clear from what was being disclosed that they felt in a desperate position and needed somebody they trusted to talk through what was happening to them.

Alarmingly, they also warned me that they felt the Conservative Party were using the police to fish for information on what they knew about problems in the local party and crucially what they had disclosed to me of goings on inside the party. As they had passed information to me, they wanted to warn me that I might be next in line for a visit from Cleveland Police.

This revelation was bad enough: that the party was now so paranoid and on the defensive that they were prepared to use the police, and criminal allegations, to silence critics and protect the party's dirty secrets.

What made it a thousand times worse was that they were doing so by targeting one of the hardest working, and most dedicated Conservative activists I had ever met. Nobody locally had done more to promote the election and re-election of local Conservative MPs and councillors than this individual. They were more committed to furthering the interests and messaging of the Conservative Party than most of the elected Tory representatives they spent many hours serving. A party which had now turned on them in the most vicious manner.

What made it truly, jaw-droppingly, repugnant, almost beyond belief, was that the party had done this when it knew the individual to be psychologically vulnerable and already dealing with a number of difficulties in their working and personal lives. Knowing that nonetheless, they had chosen to add arrest, detention in a cell, interrogation and all the other agonies of a criminal investigation into the troubled mix that was already swirling around them. And all for political motives; all to protect a desperate and unscrupulous Conservative Party

In their messages the individual concerned said that they felt bullied and humiliated, and that their treatment had been degrading. Their psychological state, already vulnerable prior to arrest, was now hurtling downwards, so much so that there was talk that the local mental health crisis team wished to admit them into inpatient care, and of them being placed on suicide watch.

At this point, my source asked me to contact CCHQ to effectively ask them to drop this matter, given the emotional and practical damage it was doing. Practical damage, because my source was unable to access email and other apps on their confiscated phone.

It's a truism that the loss of one's smart-phone is akin to social death in the modern world, so dependent have we all become on phones to manage our social lives, and in many cases, working lives, This was true in this case and made worse by the fact that the phone in question also contained apps that helped manage essential medications.

I explained that given my experience of dealing with CCHQ I didn't hold out much hope of being able to contact the right people, let alone persuade them to drop the matter. In truth I wouldn't have a clue who to try to contact, and felt I had even less chance of being successful in having the matter dropped, so far had my currency in the party dropped.

Instead I offered to contact Simon Clarke, as a one time mutual friend and as the most senior Tory MP in the region, and also a former Cabinet Minister, and this suggestion was accepted. I sent Simon the following message by text and on whatsapp:

"Hello Simon. I understand that ----------- has been arrested on suspicion of blackmail following an allegation made by -------------. ----------- is in a very fragile state psychologically and the stress of this may tip them over the edge. Please use whatever influence you have on ----------- and the party to ensure this matter is resolved with the least damage to all involved"

Given the apparent willingness of the Conservative Party to make wild allegations of blackmail against their critics, and to use the police in political disputes, and given the warnings about this from my source, I was actually afraid that I was sailing close to the wind in even making this request. Could I be accused of seeking to blackmail the party into dropping the charges by raising the prospect of 'damage to all involved'? Would Cleveland Police next be knocking on my front door to arrest me and seize my phones and laptops?

Such was my concern for the wellbeing of my source, and the damage that the Conservative Party was inflicting upon them, that it was a risk worth taking to try to restore a sense of proportion to the party's behaviour. Because I was genuinely concerned about the damage the accusations might inflict on that individual, and from the party's point of view its reputation could only be damaged if some harm did result from their behaviour.

I never received a reply from Sir Simon.

Tragically, the concerns I had about the emotional stress the party's behaviour was causing, and the risk of real harm resulting, were justified two days later when I received a text saying that my source had taken an overdose and had attempted suicide.

Thankfully the pills taken had not proved fatal and my source was under the care of the mental health crisis team, but it's a perfect example of how political calculation by the Conservative Party has dreadfully real consequences, for real people, in the real world. A consideration that too often seems forgotten in the artificial world of political scheming and strategy.

These dreadful consequences, all too often in the Conservative Party, seem to impact most damagingly on its own hardworking volunteers.

Memories of Jade Smith came flooding back; another hard working and dedicated Conservative activist let down and driven to suicide, at least in part, by her negative experiences of the way the Conservative Party treats people.

Thankfully the party did not have another suicide on its hands and its conscience, but this is what happens when pure political calculation takes place in the absence of common human decency. And as these examples demonstrate, the modern Conservative Party, and CCHQ in particular, is devoid of common human decency.

I urged my source to take it easy, to make use of the support available to them and that I was always available and just a phone call away if they felt able to speak in person.

At that point, I didn't phone my source, as I didn't want to increase the substantial pressure they were already under by forcing them to speak to me directly. If they wanted to talk, I made it clear I was available. For this reason, there existed the small chance that all these messages were part of some elaborate hoax: text messages can be faked in the way that voice phone calls cannot (AI may be changing this of course, which will open up a whole new can of worms)

There remained, at that time, the very small chance that this was a hoax undertaken by the party to discredit me, by feeding me false information and prompting me to go public with fake news, to use that horrible modern phrase. Thankfully I'm far too cautious to rush to action in anything (the age it has taken to write this book is a good example.) So this thought may just be a little bit of paranoia kicking in. Dealing with the Conservative Party can do that too.

There is also a small chance that political opponents of the Tory Party had fed me false information in all this, to get me to darken the party's name on their behalf. Mud sticks, afterall. But this seems more like paranoia too, given the further enquiries I made to check out this whole story and its source.

For the contents of the messages were entirely consistent with previous conversations I had with my source in person, they contained information known only between us, and the explanation for the new 'work' number the messages came from was entirely plausible.

Later on, after the shock of the immediate events had subsided, I traced this stated 'work' number to a business actually owned by my source. As such, I had no reasonable doubt about the provenance of the messages or the broad truth of their contents. Further enquiries and events have only strengthened that conclusion.

Crucially, I'm also aware that in all of this, I am only hearing one side of the story. No doubt the Conservative Party would put a different spin on things and I'd be delighted for them to address the allegations made in this book directly. It is open for them to do so, and I have made repeated requests for them to do so. So far they have refused.

In the meantime I had no reasonable grounds to doubt the veracity of the information supplied by my source, the troubling story it recounts, or the broad thrust of the conclusion it compels that the Conservative Party is an organisation that has lost its moral compass. An organisation that puts its own political survival above any other consideration.

Over the next few days my source and I exchanged messages, and life for them appeared to be getting back to some kind of equilibrium. Their legal representatives were highly critical of the party, the police's behaviour and the legal basis for any action at all. My source's psychological well-being improved. In due course they received their mobile phone back and in turn such a central part of everybody's life and ability to function in the modern world.

Then a strange thing happened.

My source stopped responding.

My text messages went unanswered, both to the work number they had been using and to their former usual number. Again, I didn't try calling them to speak to them directly, given their mental state, I didn't want to add to the pressure they were clearly already under. I didn't want anything I did to make them feel any worse or add to their stress levels.

If my source didn't want to speak to me now, that was fine, but it left me concerned for their welfare and puzzled as to what had gone on. Given what they had told me about the previous suicide attempt, every time there was a report of a local suicide, especially at Huntcliff (which is a disturbingly regular occurrence) my concern was renewed lest the victim eventually be named as my source.

Such was my ongoing worries that I approached Cleveland Police with a 'concern for welfare' report. To their credit they responded rapidly, made some enquiries and reported back to me that their last contact with the individual suggested they were ok.

Which begged the question of what had happened, if anything, with the allegation of blackmail made by the Conservative Party that had sparked this whole appalling episode? If my source was true, and correct, what was the police and legal resolution of the allegation? Was it proceeding? Had it been dropped? Was my source's silence the condition for the dropping of the allegation?

So many unanswered questions. All very murky, and all very disturbing.

I got in touch with other political and media contacts in the region to see if they had heard any rumours of an allegation of blackmail within the Conservative Party. The response was negative across the board.

In October 2023 I contacted the Crown Prosecution Service in the North East to ask if they were considering an allegation of blackmail that fitted with the details I had been given. In fairness to them, the CPS media contact was very helpful and confirmed that no such cases matching my description had crossed the desks of Crown Prosecutors in the region so far that year.

Which meant that either the case was still with the police, or had been dropped without charge (for whatever reason\) or the whole story was a work of fiction.

And so in October 2023 I also contacted Cleveland Police, after a couple of days I received the following response from an Officer Singh:

'Hi Lee,

Regarding your online submission. The information you are requesting is personal, and sensitive. Therefore it cannot be disclosed to you.

Regards'

An interesting response, from which one could infer that there was indeed such a case as that described by my source. The 'information's' existence wasn't denied, it simply could not be disclosed to me given that it was 'personal' and 'sensitive' It certainly wasn't a denial, and tends to confirm the broad facts alleged to me by my source as true.

Part of my reason for contacting both the CPS and Cleveland Police was not just to find out if the allegations made to me were true but also to try to avoid blundering into an ongoing criminal investigation, or perhaps worse, a prosecution.

My reply to Officer Singh made this point:

'Hello Officer Singh

Thank you for your reply.

I really just want to check that I won't be blundering into an ongoing criminal investigation if the information is correct and I raise it publicly. Given the potentially sensitive nature of a blackmail allegation this is all the more important.

Can Cleveland Police confirm whether an investigation is ongoing or not and whether it has any objection to this information being made public?

I have already contacted the CPS and they deny any knowledge of any such case.

However I do believe this is a matter of public interest if true.

Best regards

Lee Holmes'

I didn't receive a reply to this email, nor any further contact from either the CPS or Cleveland Police to date, so make of that what you will. However I'm satisfied that I've made reasonable efforts to avoid planting my size thirteens into matters of potential legal controversy. Both the CPS and police are aware of my interest in this and if there are developments towards a prosecution they know how to contact me.

The whole earlier hornet's nest of David Smith's charging with sexual offences back in 2019 have given me a natural cautiousness in blundering into the realm of sub-judice and contempt of court. But I am also motivated to make sure that voters are aware of these issues prior to any general election this year, which will be prevented if a prosecution is actually brought. These are potentially fraught circumstances all round.

The silencing of my source is also troubling. I genuinely heard every news report of a sudden death, cliff falls, bodies found in the sea or many other deaths with a sense of awful trepidation. Recently a man was struck by a train on the East Coast mainline at Thirsk, not even particularly close to this part of the world, but my first thoughts were dark worries that this might be connected. This might be the time.

It may well be that the allegations by the party were dropped, although police investigations prior to referral to the CPS can take an inordinate amount of time. Was a condition of that a requirement that my source cease all contact with me? Was the threat of a criminal prosecution used to silence a critic of the Conservative Party and its corruption? Was this threat used against an individual known to be psychologically vulnerable, with almost catastrophic results?

Has the Conservative Party employed that well worn and discredited method of a non disclosure agreement to secure the silence of yet another critic? A means of hiding the party's dirty secrets.

I don't know, despite my best efforts, warily because of the issues at stake, to uncover the truth in all this.

If this account, in this book , may prompt the truth to be made known, then it will have served its purpose.

Chapter 4 - Blackmail 2: The Minister, Volunteer, Arrest & Suicide Attempts

There have been recent developments in the arrest of the party activist on an allegation of blackmail apparently made by the Conservative Party and/or a local Conservative MP which allow me to go into more detail.

Crucially, the developments *confirm* the original story as entirely true, the small prospect of it being a hoax can now be categorically ruled out. They also make the whole troubling tale more disturbing than it first seemed, if that is possible.

So far, and true to form, the Conservative Party, and the MP concerned (now a government minister) have refused to directly address the story at all, despite numerous opportunities to do so. As such I will detail what further I know here and pursue the truth via you the reader, hopefully the press, and formal complaints to various public watchdogs to try to flush out the facts. 'Flush out' being an apt term when dealing with the sewer that the Conservative Party has become.

Early in 2024, I began recounting this particular tale on X (formerly twitter) motivated by the fear that if criminal charges were actually brought in this case then all these matters would become sub-judice and public discussion of them forbidden. With a general election possible at virtually any point I felt it was crucial to air these allegations and try to get to the truth before an election.

Of course I also had to be careful not to libel anyone, given that there remained the small possibility that these allegations were untrue. On the basis that it is quite well established law that you cannot libel a political party, I was free to make these allegations about the party rather than the particular Tory MP concerned.

Slowly, I fed the story into the public sphere, feeling my way cautiously, still concerned about revealing my source lest they had broken any bail conditions or other legal restrictions by contacting me.

People were shocked at the central assertion of the allegation, that the party could treat its own volunteers in such a way, and crucially it prompted that volunteer, my source for this story, to get back in touch with me. We arranged to meet, face to face, for the first time in nearly a year.

They confirmed everything I had previously been told and updated me on their current situation. They also asked that I not reveal their identity.

Thankfully the blackmail allegation had eventually, after several weeks of tremendous upset and stress, been dropped by Cleveland Police without charges being brought. Though it was apparently dropped with the subtle threat that the matter had been dropped 'for now.'

Shockingly, the stress of the initial arrest and subsequent events had led to *six* suicide attempts by my source, and although they were receiving support it was clear that the allegation made by the party had had an appalling effect on their physical and mental health and their entire life and livelihood. A real world victim of the Conservative Party's amoral political scheming.

Interestingly, my source informed me that the MP at the centre of the allegation had apparently been interviewed with a solicitor present, which is extremely odd given they were either the complainant in the case or merely a witness. Why have a solicitor present at all?

Now I can also reveal that this MP is Jacob Young, Conservative member for Redcar constituency and now Under Secretary of State for Levelling Up, Housing and Communities.

Was this solicitor a Conservative Party lawyer and were the party, as such, effectively directing the investigation? Political interference in a police investigation of what was effectively a purely political dispute anyway. In 2023. In the United Kingdom.

My source recounted that the arresting officer used the phrase 'with malice' when describing the alleged offence of blackmail that he was being arrested for. Now this in particular is odd, as the presence or otherwise of 'malice' is utterly irrelevant in the offence of blackmail as detailed by Section 21 of the Theft Act 1968. It simply doesn't come into the offence, so this begs the question where this phrase had come from? Had it been raised by the solicitor present at the MP's interview?

In the complaint we raised about the arrest, which also confirmed all the details of the arrest as true, the reviewing officer also uses this mysterious and irrelevant phrase about blackmail 'with malice'. That Cleveland Police don't understand the law they are arresting citizens under is disturbing enough, but not perhaps surprising, but once again, who has put this phrase into the officer's minds? Was someone effectively directing the arrest for political purposes?

A contact in the regional press had taken up my allegations on X and had contacted Cleveland Police about them. At that stage they would do no more than confirm that an arrest had been made but that charges had never been brought and the investigation had been closed.

As such, that had also confirmed the central story as true.

My own repeated contacts to the Conservative Party, their Press Office both locally and nationally, the Conservative Party National Convention Chairman Peter Booth (a man with particular responsibility for the volunteers in the party) and the Jacob Young MP have elicited no responses. No denials.

The only contact I have had from the party was from its Chief of Staff offering an internal safeguarding review of the case. For the party to investigate itself. This I politely declined.

All this begs the question of who made the initial complaint to police in the first place?

Who felt that having a hardworking and vulnerable party volunteer arrested on an allegation of blackmail in what was a purely political dispute was the right way to go? Morally and politically.

Whodunnit? If you like.

Was it the MP at the centre of the dispute? Jacob Young MP, now a junior minister in government (though given the Conservative chaos of the last few years there are few MPs who haven't been a junior minister at some point) A self avowedly devout Christian. Also a long term friend of the activist so shabbily treated.

Was it Jacob Young who made the complaint to the police and had a long standing friend and hard working volunteer arrested?

Or was it the party centrally, in response to a contact by that MP?

It is unlikely to have been a member of staff in that MP's office who would take it upon themselves to make such a serious criminal complaint to police.

But did that MP discuss it with them or others in the local party?

Was it ever raised by the MP with our local Police and Crime Commissioner, who was the subject, at least in part, of the dispute over selections in the local elections, and also concerns over alleged staff problems in offices that he previously ran for the local MP?

Certainly PCC Steve Turner has 'form' when it comes to raising complaints against critics with his own police force, as you will see in the following chapter.

This is pure conjecture, of course, and I am accusing nobody in particular in the absence of all the facts. But a criminal complaint was undoubtedly made.

And in an election year, with voters about to elect those who govern them, and on the fundamental belief that they have a right to know what they are voting for, I will keep looking for the truth.

For now, and with the permission of the victim in all this, who still wishes to remain anonymous, that will be through complaints to the Parliamentary Standards Commissioner regarding the behaviour of the MP, and if necessary to the IOPC with regard to the police investigation.

In the latest development a complaint about the arrest made through the formal police complaints system has found that the legal grounds for the arrest of the volunteer, utterly devastating as it was, were not clearly established and may not have been present at all. The reason for the repeated use of the phrase 'with malice' was also found to be unfounded and problematic. We will be pursuing these matters further.

The Conservative Party and Jacob Young MP are, true to form, refusing to disclose the truth in this whole sorry affair, but there are other ways to shine a light on it.

And daylight, as they say, is the strongest disinfectant.

Chapter 5 - The Police and *Crime* Commissioner

By May 2023 the narrative detailed in this book had been overtaken by truly extraordinary events in Conservative politics. Nationally, we saw the death throes of the Johnson premiership, where Boris, finally caught out by his natural instinct to lie, was brought down by Conservative MPs no longer willing to go out and man the media barricades armed only with Boris' peculiar version of the truth. By the end of those fevered days in summer 2022 it seemed as if Johnson had offered a cabinet position to everyone in Downing Street, including the cleaners and Larry the Cat (who declined)

The Johnson defenestration was followed by a Conservative Party leadership campaign that exhibited all the worst aspects of the party membership's sentiments, as members opted for the low-quality Thatcher tribute act Truss over the organised, but limited, Sunak.

As discussed elsewhere, the fact that Truss clearly was not Thatcher, both in her character and policy positions, and that this was pointed out by numerous senior Conservatives who had actually worked with Margaret Thatcher, didn't seem to matter to a clear majority of Tory members. Instead, they settled for comforting nostalgia over competence and economic reality.

The Truss debacle was so brief that it barely merits a chapter of its own, but so extraordinary and instructive as to the nature of the Conservative Party's problems is it, that a chapter it does get. Suffice to say that the chaos of the Johnson/Truss/Sunak days of

2022 made me grateful to have left the party, for to defend that shambles I simply couldn't.

Locally, here in that favoured corner of Johnson's 'Levelling-Up' agenda, Teesside, we witnessed less reported-upon, but almost as troubling and extraordinary, events in Conservative politics.

In particular, I personally witnessed the spectacle of a serving Conservative Police and Crime Commissioner calling in his own police force to investigate his critics and political opponents during an election campaign. For readers, I was one of those critics investigated.

Such an intervention as dragging the police into a purely political dispute may seem more at home in Vladimir Putin's Russia, rather than Cleveland in North East England. But it seems that the current Conservative Party is developing a taste for it.

It raises serious questions about conflicts of interest, misuse of police resources and anti-democratic attempts to shut down legitimate political debate. However, I've long since ceased to be surprised by events in this part of the world, or the modern Conservative Party for that matter.

So, how did we get here?

I'd known Steve Turner, current (at time of writing) Police and Crime Commissioner for Cleveland Police, since 2019 when I became Deputy Chairman Political of South Tees Conservatives. At this time Steve was constituency office manager for Simon Clarke MP. Steve had previously been a Ukip councillor locally, and regional chairman of the Vote Leave campaign during the EU Referendum in 2016. He had defected to the Conservative Party when its own shift onto Ukip territory had caused Nigel Farage's original variety to implode.

Steve always struck me as a competent manager for Simon Clarke, having as he did a long previous career in management in the retail sector (more on this, crucially, coming up.) He also seemed to have a sound political judgement and we always got on well on a personal level whenever our respective duties overlapped, which was often.

His relationship with Simon Clarke was close, troublingly so. It often seemed that what Steve wanted, Steve got when it came to Simon. It appeared to me, in earlier days at least, that Steve and his wife Andrea had some kind of hold over Simon, given that they so often seemed to benefit from decisions taken by the latter.

Now I'm not suggesting for a moment anything improper, let alone illegal, in this relationship, but it always struck me as odd. This willingness of Simon to accommodate Turner's wishes and interests may merely have stemmed from Simon being an inexperienced new MP, a bit wet behind the ears, and dependent upon an older and hardier politician in Steve Turner.

In conversation with Andy Preston, former Independent Mayor of Middlesbrough who knew both men well, it was suggested that Steve's working class bruiser persona was a valuable foil to Simon's public-school poshboy personality, and this probably has some truth to it as well.

It may also have had something to do with the fact that Turner, standing for Ukip, had helped to deprive Simon's predecessor as wannabe MSEC Tory MP, Will Goodhand, of victory over Labour at the 2015 election. Turner's defection to the Tories and failure to stand again in 2017 undoubtedly helped Simon's election, and maybe there was some kind of quid pro quo deal. Or maybe Simon merely felt indebted to Turner for his election. The fact they undoubtedly shared strong Brexiteer views, and other strident views on the right of Tory politics, maybe also led Clarke to be more accommodating of Turner than might have been the case otherwise.

Interestingly this dependence on the Turners was later repeated by Jacob Young on his becoming Redcar's first ever Tory MP in 2019, with Steve Turner becoming Jacob's office manager whilst also continuing as Simon's chief of staff. Andrea Turner, Steve's wife, was also taken on by Jacob as a senior constituency caseworker. This arrangement though didn't last, and by all accounts didn't end well.

As Chairman of South Tees Conservatives at the time, I had misgivings about this apparent monopolising of power by the Turners, over both our local Tory MPs. It did however seem to make sense, given that Turner had recent experience from Simon's election in 2017 of setting up and running a constituency office from scratch. As it turns out (more on this later) the closeness of these relationships was not to last, and would sour considerably in a short time.

The most shocking element in the story of Steve Turner as Cleveland Police and Crime Commissioner, among many, was also the cause for my falling out with him: the fact that when he put himself forward to be a Conservative PCC he failed to disclose the small matter that he had previously accepted a police caution for thieving from a former employer. This criminal act, to many people, not least myself, would be regarded as making a person wholly unsuitable for the role of a Police and Crime Commissioner.

Turner has consistently failed to come clean about the full circumstances of this caution. When, in late 2021, Middlesbrough's Labour MP Andy McDonald initially accused Turner of being sacked for 'systematic theft' from a previous employer when in a managerial role, using parliamentary privilege to do so, Turner's first response was outright denial. This was arguably a further act of serious public dishonesty by a Police and Crime Commissioner.

Some time later Turner finally admitted to accepting a police caution approximately 20 years ago for 'handling stolen goods to a value of £15' whilst employed as a manager for Safeway supermarkets. This was purely Turner's account of events, for no official record has ever been released. He claimed in his defence not to have been sacked by his employer but to have resigned. The phrase 'jumping before one is pushed' springs to mind and it's an odd line of defence to take.

Turner has never clearly said whether the goods were stolen from his employer, which would make the offence all the more serious. The fact he hasn't denied this suggests it was indeed the case.

The limited admission given was clearly an attempt to diminish the seriousness of his criminal behaviour: he hadn't stolen anything himself, but *merely* handled stolen goods after their theft by someone else. Though arguably, handling stolen goods is akin to conspiring with somebody else to facilitate thieving, which if anything is worse than mere theft. To most right-thinking people.

Turner made much of the fact he had merely accepted a police caution rather than being convicted, and crucially this does make an important difference to his qualification to be a PCC. Had he been prosecuted and convicted of this offence he WOULD have been disqualified from running to be a PCC. It's worth remembering that at the time of Turner's caution, police were notorious for seeking to increase crime clear-up rates and cut the use of CPS and court resources by offering cautions for serious offences that really should have been prosecuted. In this, Turner really did strike lucky.

Turner's failure to disclose that caution, and the criminality behind it, either to the party in his PCC application, or to voters during the election, or to myself when tapping me up for a substantial donation to his campaign, was a further act of serious dishonesty. In any sane world that pattern of dishonest behaviour should rule Turner out from being placed in charge of any police force.

It should be noted, in fairness to Turner, that he was apparently under no legal obligation to disclose his previous police caution in applying to become a PCC candidate or indeed a PCC.

Somewhat bizarrely the Rehabilitation of Offenders Act rules do not expect Police and Crime Commissioners to be held to the 'utmost integrity' standards that require full disclosure of ANY previous contact with the police. These rules DO apply to anyone hoping to become a police constable, paid or volunteer, but apparently don't apply to people wanting to be in charge of those police constables. Odd.

This may have been an oversight by our politicians in drafting the rules, but surely 'utmost integrity' is something we should be aiming for in elected public officials, not least those in charge of local policing? Given the state of our politics under characters such as Boris Johnson and others in the Conservative Party maybe I'm being naive to believe that 'utmost integrity' is still a feature in British public life. It should be, however.

I should make clear, as well, that I'm all in favour of the concept and practice of rehabilitation; people do deserve a second, and possibly even a third, chance (bleeding-heart liberal that I am!) But honesty, in my mind, is central to the process of rehabilitation, especially in public life, and Turner's failure to disclose his past criminality to anyone is a black mark of dishonesty almost as bad as his (very serious) initial criminally dishonest behaviour.

A system of disqualification from being a PCC so strict that it infamously excluded Falklands War hero Simon Weston from standing, due to some minor criminality as a *juvenile*, should surely have excluded Turner for serious criminal dishonesty committed as an adult against his employer. This was a serious breach of the law, and of trust.

As it was, Turner's failure to mention the small matter of stealing from his employer while in a managerial position, meant that voters didn't get a chance to pass judgement on whether or not a thief should be a Police and Crime Commissioner. Turner was elected in May 2021 alongside Tees Valley Mayor Ben Houchen in an election delayed by a year due to covid restrictions. His victory was in no small part due to running on the same ticket, at the same election, as the then very popular Ben Houchen.

(Interestingly, it has been suggested that Turner's caution for handling stolen goods, even if 'spent', should have been flagged up on the criminal records check for his Parliamentary security clearance to be Simon Clarke's constituency office manager. The suggestion is that Simon Clarke should have been aware of Turner's criminal background when putting him in charge of dealing with constituent's sensitive personal matters as his office manager, in providing him with a reference to be a Conservative PCC candidate, in pulling strings when his application was initially rejected (see below) and in publicly supporting Turner in his campaign to be elected as PCC in 2021.

If this is not the case, and I have offered Clarke and Turner plenty of opportunities to clarify, or deny, this matter, and am doing so again here, I will happily correct the record. For it would be a pretty shocking state of affairs for an MP and one time Cabinet Minister to allegedly be prepared to participate in deceiving others, including voters, about the suitability of someone to be a Police and Crime Commissioner.

If correct, the apparent extent to which Clarke would go to aid Turner is troubling, to say the least. Whether Clarkes's provision of a reference for Turner in his application to be a Conservative PCC candidate, in such circumstances, would amount to illegality is a question for better lawyers than myself, but, if true, would be at least a moral black mark against the behaviour and judgement of this one-time Cabinet member.

Clarke's reference for Turner also led to his stock at CCHQ falling through the floor, which turned out to be unfortunate for others dependent on his 'good word' as a referee. Not least me.)

In what turned out to be a landslide victory for a clearly still very popular Houchen, up against a poor choice for Labour candidate Jessie Jacobs, Turner very much coasted into power on Ben's coat tails. Ben Houchen had been elected first in 2017 in a surprise result, beating Labour's candidate for the Mayoralty Sue Jeffries on second preference votes. His high-energy, high-promise tenure since, coupled with the fact Teesside and he himself had become the posterboy for Boris Johnson's 'Levelling Up' agenda, meant that there was never very much doubt that Ben would be elected in 2021, and that Turner was likely to be elected on the same ticket.

Turner's chances were also helped by the fact that the Labour predecessor in the role of Cleveland PCC, Barry Coppinger, was widely regarded as ineffectual in the job and had left under something of a cloud about potential misuse of police resources. Ironically, this was in investigating Steve Turner.

The fact that Labour's chosen replacement for Coppinger, Dr Paul Williams, former MP for Stockton South until 2019, had very late in the day decided to jump ship from the PCC candidacy to run as Labour's candidate for the Hartlepool parliamentary by-election can't have harmed Turner's chances either. It certainly did nothing for Williams political career, however, as he lost in a shock result as the Tories claimed Hartlepool for the first time.

The assistance that South Tees Conservatives gave to Turner, as one of our own, also can't have harmed his election chances. Turner asked me as Chairman to propose a donation from the association towards his campaign and I was happy to do so, being ignorant of his criminal past at the time. I secured a not insubstantial £1000 donation with my Executive Council's agreement towards Turner's campaign fund and it was more than matched by CCHQ in return.

I occasionally wish that I had asked Turner at the time whether there was anything in his current life, or background, that might cause embarrassment to the association in making a donation to him.

Foolishly, I trusted that the vetting process supposedly carried out by the CCHQ Candidates Team would have turned up such small matters as police cautions for serious criminal dishonesty, and never posed the question to him. Had I done so, an honest answer from Turner would have seen the donation denied, and quite possibly I would have felt compelled to go public with the information of his criminality before the vote, which would no doubt have led to a very different result. A dishonest answer on the other hand may well have left Turner open to a charge of fraud, given that it's not clear that the Rehabilitation of Offenders Act would apply to such a transaction.

As it is, I never asked, and life is often a long list of 'what ifs'.

Quite apart from the financial backing I secured for Turner I personally delivered literally thousands of leaflets promoting both him and Ben Houchen in the run up to the elections in 2021, and alongside our Deputy Chairman Political helped to organise other delivery teams to get the message out there. The sense of betrayal when the truth came out is all the more sickening given the personal effort put in, and that's as true for Turner as it is of my work for the Conservative Party generally.

So, how did we get to the situation in 2023 when a serving Police and Crime Commissioner called in his own police force to investigate his own political critics?

Between his May 2021 election, and May 2023 Turner weathered a storm of complaints made to the local policing panel about his conduct, both past and present. Allegations relating to the proven theft from his employer and failure to disclose this, and unproven allegations of historic sexual and physical assaults, came and went and nothing was found to bar him from his position as PCC.

I myself as Chairman of STCA at the time of such allegations had to ask my Executive Council whether we should suspend Turner's Conservative Party membership pending the outcome of enquiries, after prompting from members of the local party. Correctly, as it turned out, we all unanimously decided against doing so. 'Innocent until proven guilty' is still a principle that needs defending, even in these cancel-culture days.

By early 2023 it appeared that Turner had weathered the storm, all such complaints coming to nothing. At this point Turner made the really curious, and as it turned out utterly foolish, decision to stand for Redcar and Cleveland Borough Council in the May local elections.

The sight of a serving Police and Crime Commissioner for one of the worst performing, and most troubled, police forces in the country, which at the time was still in special measures, deciding to run for the local council looked odd at best. At worst it looked greedy and entitled.

Shouldn't a PCC for such a dysfunctional force be busy getting on with the day job? I certainly thought so and, as it turned out, so did many others, not least voters in the ward Turner chose to stand in. Even more so when that PCC has such a chequered past, one which many felt should have disqualified him from the PCC role in the first place.

The fact that the next election for Cleveland PCC falls in 2024, just a year away after the term was cut short by the covid-delayed election of 2021, and that Turner is highly likely to lose, probably motivated him to want to get his feet under another local government table as an insurance policy. That was the plan anyway...

Whatever the motive (and maybe it is an *overwhelmingly* strong sense of public service) the move proved politically inept and disastrous, as was entirely predictable beforehand. Such foolishness might be forgiven and, for the record, until this point I had always regarded Turner as being quite politically astute, but he compounded the political idiocy by standing in the same ward as his wife Andrea. This would be bad enough in itself, but they did so in

Longbeck where Andrea had been a sitting Tory councillor in a two member ward alongside independent, and former Conservative, Vera Rider (much more on this elsewhere)

As an association we learned from experience in the 2019 local elections, and I also touch on this elsewhere, that standing two or more Conservative candidates in a multi-member ward with a popular incumbent Independent usually meant splitting the Conservative vote, and risked getting fewer of your Tory candidates elected.

Saltburn Ward in 2019 was a case in point: a three member ward with a popular independent going for re-election. CCHQ and the Regional Campaign Manager insisted we stand three Conservative candidates, one of whom was only a paper candidate anyway, and in doing so we split the Conservative vote and only got one Conservative elected. (Conservative inclined voters having three votes had used one for the popular Independent and then split their other two votes among the three Tory candidates, thus splitting Tory support.)

The second Tory candidate in that case was Jacob Young, who at least had the consolation of unexpectedly becoming an MP later the same year.

So for both Turner's to stand in a ward with a popular Independent incumbent seemed like mission impossible to get *both* elected, and as it turned out, neither made it across the finish line.

I understand from sources still in the local party that Andrea had insisted upon Steve standing with her in Longbeck Ward and this may well be true. One suggestion is that Andrea wanted to be the first Tory candidate on the ballot paper alphabetically in order to pick up more Tory votes, and Steve gave her this advantage compared to the other potential candidate.

I also have it on good authority that the selection failed to follow Conservative Party rules and that dark threats of defection to the independents may have been floating around in order to get the joint Turner ticket approved. If true, that makes the final result all the more delicious. Schadenfreude is my favourite German word.

For it was my hand in assisting this result, through my public criticism of Turner's decision to stand at all, and the Labour Party's use of that, that seemed to upset PCC Turner, and lead to him calling in Cleveland Police to deal with us.

This sorry saga of political butt-hurt and police interference in legitimate political debate began with criticism I made of Steve Turner on twitter (now X). This initially focused on his dishonesty with voters and others in not declaring his police caution for handling stolen goods. The tweets were critical, highly so at times, and drawing attention to uncomfortable truths about Steve Turner's behaviour and other issues of public interest in the local Conservative Party. Turner would later accuse me of running a 'hate-filled campaign' against him, and on that basis called in his own police force to investigate my tweets.

You can draw your own conclusions from the tweets about whether there was any 'hate' involved, Cleveland Police, once called in, certainly felt not:

(My tweets **in bold below** are almost all the tweets I made on the subject, two or three haven't been reproduced due to irrelevance or duplication. They were tweeted over many months and amongst many, many other tweets on many other different subjects, but taken together in a long list look may look a little obsessive on my part. But I'm not, honestly!)

May 2022, a tweet from my twitter account, a whole year before the complaint, to give some idea of the nature and duration of my criticism:

"A caution is an acceptance of criminal guilt to avoid prosecution. In Steve Turner's case for thieving from his employer. He then compounded THAT dishonesty by withholding that inconvenient fact from local party members and voters. Is that appropriate behaviour for a PCC?"

The above, and the following tweets, were in reply to a Guido Fawkes tweet about Turner criticising others for dishonesty for making allegations against him. They also raise my concerns about the failure of Conservative vetting processes to turn up that caution.

"Is this the Conservative PCC with a police caution for handling stolen goods in his background?
Could you ask the Conservative Party how he was ever allowed to be a candidate for the 'party of law & order'.
I've tried, as his former association Chairman, but they won't tell me."

"Steve Turner asked local voters to put him in charge of the local police force only last year, and failed to tell them about criminal activity in his past. IMO that's a continuation of the dishonesty that saw him cautioned for stealing from his employer."

These tweets raised no response from Turner or the Guido Fawkes account, though did lead someone on twitter to accuse me of being dangerously radical, to which I replied:

"A brief look at my timeline shows I dislike the dishonesty of senior politicians breaking the law and then lying about it, whether that's Boris Johnson or Steve Turner. There's a pattern here. Actually I'm boringly establishment usually. I just despise corruption."

Also in 2022 the following tweets were sent in response to feverish speculation, by journalist Michael Crick among others, that in the meltdown of Boris Johnson's administration in July 2022, Simon Clarke MP was about to be promoted to Chancellor of the Exchequer.

I raised the concerns I had as his former association chairman about both Simon's judgement and probity:

"I understand that Simon pulled strings within the party to have his office manager Steve Turner's application for the party's PCC candidate list approved, following its initial rejection. Mr Turner is now a PCC with a police caution for stealing from his employer on his record." (Reply to Michael Crick)

Michale Crick asked for further details, but seemed unaware of precisely who Steve Turner is. Fame eh?

My responses to Crick:

"When I put this accusation to Simon he certainly didn't deny it. Poor judgement. Possible undue influence. Major embarrassment for the party when Turner's background uncovered."

"I'm saying it because I put it to Simon and he didn't deny it. Which seems odd. I also asked CCHQ for an explanation of how the party came to have someone with Steve Turner's past criminality as a PCC candidate, and they wouldn't explain ½"

"My evidence on this is not hearsay btw: I put it to Simon that he had intervened to change the rejection of Steve Turner's PCC application and he responded not by denying that, but by claiming he had tried to do the same for me! I have screenshots of this."

This issue was taken up in the local press earlier that year and the only response we got from Clarke was that Turner had been rejected on technical grounds, not his police caution, which the party seemed unaware of. Simon claimed that a popular appeal by lots of local Conservatives in support of Turner had led to that rejection being overturned. I've yet to come across any such local Conservatives involved in overturning Turner's rejection other than Clarke himself. I was also contacted by another local association Chair who also vehemently rejected Simon's version of events.

Further tweets on the issue of quite how Steve Turner came to be a Conservative PCC candidate despite apparently being rejected by the party initially, also July 2022:

"@SimonClarkeMP As you put Steve Turner in charge of local constituent's affairs as your constituency manager presumably YOU did due diligence on his background? What did you know about his criminal past before intervening to help him become PCC?"

Strangely, I'm now blocked by Simon Clarke's twitter account.

As stated above, if Turner went through parliamentary clearance as Clarke's office manager his criminal records check *should* have flagged up the police caution and Simon Clarke *should* have been aware of it.

The following tweet was in response to the local press coverage of my allegation that Turner had initially been rejected by the party for its PCC candidates list, but had mysteriously been accepted following an intervention by Simon Clarke. In the article Clarke claimed that 'Conservatives from across the region' had intervened to support Turner's cause.

"**More questions than answers in Simon's response. And no denial. Who were these 'Conservatives from across the Cleveland Police region' who intervened to have Steve Turner's PCC rejection overturned?**"

This has never been answered, of course.

The following is some gentle trolling from Oct 2022, following the debacle of the Liz Truss micro-premiership, and Simon Clarke apparently backing a return for Boris Johnson, just weeks after his sacking by Tory MPs simply exhausted by his serial dishonesty:

"**Simon Clarke really can pick 'em:**

Liz Truss

Steve Turner, the Cleveland Police and Crime Commissioner, and Simon's former office manager, who has a police caution for stealing from a former employer.

And now Boris (again)
What could possibly go wrong?
#Conservatives"

As you can see it's political criticism, requests for answers and some gentle, humorous trolling, but hardly merits a police investigation so far.

Several months later and the issue of Steve Turner's behaviour and criminal background came to the fore again following his (to my mind, quite extraordinary and foolish) decision to stand for the local council in Apr 2023:

"Surprised that Cleveland Police & Crime Commissioner Steve Turner feels the need to be a councillor too. Complaints within the local party also that Conservative Party selection rules were broken in choosing Steve. Why am I not surprised"

The above tweet referenced allegations from reliable sources within the local party that party rules had been broken in Steve Turner's selection. By this stage I was of course no longer South Tees Chairman and it seems the old bad habits of gerrymandered selections had returned.

Next a little more gentle trolling, that no doubt chimed with a lot of hard pressed locals:

"We're all struggling with the cost of living crisis but does our Cleveland Police PCC Steve Turner really need a extra 10 grand a year from hard pressed taxpayers on top of his £80,000 PCC salary? #Conservatives"

The following tweet referenced the allegation I received that Councillor Andrea Turner, Steve's wife and the Conservative Group Leader on RCBC was suing her employer, Simon Clarke MP. The source I had for this was likewise reliable and included a whatsapp message from Simon Clarke himself that stated that his relationship with Andrea was now 'litigious'. Straight from the horse's mouth as it were.

I hasten to add, that I would never usually mention the spouses or family of political opponents unless they were involved in politics themselves, as was the case with Andrea as Tory Group leader.

In addition, the suggestion that the Conservative Group leader on the local council was suing a local Conservative MP *was* undoubtedly a matter of public interest, especially at election time as the party seeks to put forward a united front, and the fact that taxpayers were likely to have to fund any settlement of the action. (Steve Turner later replied to deny there was any such legal action, which is odd as Simon Clarke had effectively confirmed it.)

"Can it really be the case that the Conservative Group Leader on Redcar & Cleveland Council, Andrea Turner (wife of our esteemed PCC) is SUING local Conservative MP Simon Clarke?

Reputable sources say it is.

Local Conservatives are as dysfunctional as the party nationally"

Having also raised the issue with contacts in the local press, it appeared everyone in the Conservative Party was 'keeping mum' so to speak:

**"I understand Clarke is taking a 'no comment' response to media enquiries. The hope seems to be a pay-off with a gagging clause (presumably paid for with taxpayers money) to keep us all in the dark.
The usual poison in Conservative Party politics"**

"Interestingly, Mrs Turner previously left the employment of Jacob Young MP, under a similar cloud, and was immediately accommodated by Simon Clarke MP.
The Turner's seem, in my opinion, to have some kind of hold over our local MPs
All very odd."

At this point Steve Turner popped up on twitter with this denial (complete with emojis)

"Simply not true I'm afraid lee. Andrea had a contract with both MPs since Jacob's election in 2019. It was part of a joint Office arrangement between the MPs.

Your "source" has seriously let you down. 🤦 "

My reply, slightly mischievous but encouraged that we might actually get some answers on these issues:

"Hi Steve, thanks for the clarification. Can you confirm whether Andrea is suing Simon Clarke, Jacob Young, both, or neither?"

To which Steve replied:

"I can confirm your info is duff there too"

Short, succinct, but news to Simon who certainly seemed to think he was being sued by Andrea, given the whatsapp message he had sent to my source, as my reply somewhat cheekily made out:

"That's strange because Simon was certainly under the impression he was being sued by Mrs Turner.

He will be relieved…"

Further tweet as new information became available about the rather odd candidate selection choice in Longbeck:

"Latest on the Longbeck selection dispute: PCC Steve Turner was apparently selected ahead of a long standing Conservative member who actually lives in the ward & would have been a strong local candidate. Mrs Turner voted in the selection, in breach of party rules."

Further criticism of a PCC standing for the local council instead of getting on with the job of running a truly troubled police force:

"It is shocking that PCC Steve Turner is standing to be a councillor when Cleveland Police is in such a mess. But tbh I've ceased to be shocked or surprised by goings-on in the Conservative Party"

General criticism focused mostly on Simon Clarke's judgement but referencing Turner's record of dishonesty:

"It must be said that Simon Clarke MP, who IS otherwise an intelligent guy, has a real talent for backing losers, whether that's Boris, Liz Truss, Boris again, and not forgetting Steve Turner, our light-fingered PCC, whose initial rejection Clarke pulled strings to overturn"

In response to replies to my tweets I revisited the allegation of a legal action:

"Yes this IS strange, given that PCC Steve Turner denied there was any legal action against Simon Clarke on here just 2 days ago.
Taxpayers and voters have a right to know if their local MP is paying out to a local councillor, how much, and what for. It's our money afterall"

"Yes very odd that Simon Clarke MP says he is being sued by the Turners but Steve Turner denies it on here. Voters have a right to know what's going on and whether they are paying for it"

In other tweets about the local Conservative Party I mentioned that a member I had previously had to warn about offensive social media posts, when Chairman, had been selected to be a Conservative Party local election candidate (with the full knowledge of the local party and MPs of that background) This individual was a close friend of the Turners, as were many other local party candidates in May 2023

Those social media posts had referred to those having abortions, and the doctors providing them, as 'baby murderers'. I made a point of not naming them, the point was a general indication of the way the party had swung to the right politically, but the individual had then outed themselves on facebook, possibly at Turner's behest to ensure he wasn't mistakenly thought to be the source of the comments.

The candidate had also espoused various extreme covid conspiracy theories and opinions on social media during the pandemic.

A tweet commenting on the furore which had now made the local press:

"Disappointed there's been no response from the Conservative Party or local Tory MPs to their candidate's 'baby murderer' views, or the apparent legal action by a Tory councillor against Simon Clarke MP, or PCC Steve Turner running for council when he's got a job to do.
To recap.."

"before we move onto the really serious stuff:
PCC Steve Turner was selected in breach of Conservative Party rules to run for RCBC, rather than getting on with his £80,000 a year job tackling a scandal hit police force.
This despite withholding his criminal background to be PCC"

"And despite the apparent fact, stated by Simon Clarke MP, that Clarke was being sued by Andrea Turner, wife of Steve, and Leader of the Conservative group on RCBC…"

"Meanwhile, as sound long-time Conservative members were been rejected in favour of Turner as council candidates, a close friend of the Turners, Stephen Cargill, was selected as a candidate despite appalling views on COVID and abortion, which were known by the local party and MPs"

"I've thought for a long time that our local Conservative MPs seemed in thrall to the Turners: what the Turners want, the Turners seem to get.
Now it seems they and the local party are frightened of the Turners. Which begs the question why?"

"If you're hoping for answers from the Conservative Party you'll be disappointed: their approach is always silence, denial, cover-up.
But the Turner dimension is the least of the scandals in the local Conservative Party and I'll be saying more later today."

(The further details promised covered the earlier selection of David Smith and alleged prior knowledge of his offending, as detailed in Chapter 2)

A further tweet on whether PCC Steve Turner should be getting on with his police and crime role in response to new reports on local crime:

"Middlesbrough has the 2nd highest burglary rate in England. Shouldn't Cleveland Police PCC Steve Turner be getting on with his day job rather than running for council? #ConservativeParty"

In response to a facebook post by Turner accusing his detractors of being 'hateful' I tweeted the following alongside a screenshot of his post:

"Turner needs to be careful accusing his detractors of being 'hateful'.

I'm not motivated by hate but an opposition to dishonesty (criminal in Steve's case), greed and arrogance, which can only be the motivation for a PCC seeking an extra 10 grand as a councillor."

A tweet accompanying a facebook picture of Steve Turner in Harry Potter fancy dress for a witches and wizards halloween party that he went ahead with on the same day that a Conservative MP was brutally murdered:

"The thing about Steve Turner is he's happy to be a Conservative Police & Crime Commissioner when it suits but less so if it's inconvenient, as here (as Harry Potter) when he went ahead with a party on the day Tory MP Sir David Amess was brutally murdered."

In response to a tweet about the PCC's office hiring yet more clerical staff

"Maybe PCC Steve Turner will send a PR executive to deal with your burglary?"

A general criticism of the relationship between Turner and our local MPs:

"There's a very strange relationship between both our local Conservative MPs and the PCC, it always seemed to me that what Mr Turner wants, he gets. Including praise it seems."

So far, as you can see, my tweets are a mixture of political criticism, raising of disturbing questions and a fair bit of light-hearted, humorous trolling (I'm only human)

It appears by this stage of the election campaign Turner was aware things were not going well and his ire was spilling over onto his facebook campaign page, on which he claimed I was being investigated for 'harassing' him. This was news to me, though apparently referred to his own complaint, to his own police force, about my tweets critical of him and his decision to stand:

"Right. I've been in conversation with PCC Steve Turner, asking him to take down & retract the accusation against me of 'harassment'. Harassment is a criminal offence and a very serious matter. Public scrutiny of political candidates in a democracy is absolutely NOT harassment ½"

"Unfortunately, Mr Turner has declined to do so, so I'll be taking legal advice.
I also want voters to know of recent conduct by Mr Turner which is utterly unbecoming a PCC, which previously I haven't disclosed on the grounds of taste"

As my above tweet stated, I had been sent a whatsapp message from Steve Turner to a local resident who Turner knew to be vulnerable. I was so shocked by the nature of the message and its subject matter that, on the grounds of taste, I had simply sat on it and not publicised it. However if Turner was going to go down the route of accusing me of harassment then the gloves were off, and voters deserved to know what he was capable of:

"This message from PCC Steve Turner to a vulnerable individual (not me) is emotional blackmail of the lowest order, utterly unethical, and unbecoming a Police & Crime Commissioner. I've withheld it on the grounds of decency but enough is enough"

The screen shot accompanying the tweet showed Turner sending an unsolicited message to a local resident who was a source of some of the information I had received. Turner knew, or must have known, that this individual was vulnerable and he clearly knew that they had previously lost someone to suicide. In it Turner said the following:

"As someone who lost someone they loved and cared for I wanted you to know that your and Lee's hate filled campaign against us will potentially cost another life. I hope you can sleep at night."

"Tonight I'm calling for the immediate resignation of Cleveland Police PCC Steve Turner and will be following up with a formal complaint to the Local Policing Panel. This behaviour is completely unacceptable"

I did refer the whatsapp message sent by Turner mentioning suicide to the Local Policing Panel, questioning also whether the message breached the law under the Malicious Communications Act, Their legal advice taken was that it didn't breach the law, which is odd to say the least, but that it was inappropriate for a PCC to be sending such a message. They recommended that Turner should receive social media training, which demonstrates just how toothless scrutiny of PCCs can be.

Most shockingly of all, the recipient of that threatening message from PCC Steve Turner was, within days, arrested by Turner's own police force, on an allegation made by Turner's pal Jacob Young MP, and/or the Conservative Party. That arrest, devastating as it was to a person already struggling, led to numerous suicide attempts. Turner's threats were certainly prophetic.

Turner's behaviour and resulting treatment is a stark contrast with the example of a neighbouring Police and Crime Commissioner for North Yorkshire Police as I pointed out in the following tweet:

"It's worth noting that the former North Yorkshire PCC Philip Allott resigned over foolish comments about the murder of Sarah Everard. Here we have the Cleveland PCC Steve Turner attempting emotional blackmail of a vulnerable individual who had previously lost someone to suicide"

A few days later:

"I've today made a formal complaint about Cleveland Police PCC Steve Turner's unethical, unprofessional (and possibly illegal) emotional blackmail against a local critic. Maybe @Conservatives should take action too"

"Btw in case people think I'm a serial complainer about the PCC, I've only previously made one complaint: whether Mr Turner failing to declare his police caution to me (when procuring a donation) or the Conservative Party was fraudulent? (Apparently not, according to the IOPC)"

As things hotted-up further in the election campaign and Turner clearly got wind that things weren't going his way, he contacted me on whatsapp to say that he had made a complaint to Cleveland Police about my twitter criticism of him.

"You should know I've been threatened with a police investigation by PCC Steve Turner into whether I've told untruths about him as an election candidate (I haven't) BUT I'D WELCOME THIS, as it would entail an investigation into all the Conservative Party corruption I'm detailing."

After I received a telephone call from Cleveland Police confirming that they had received a complaint from Turner, and had investigated it but could see no cause for action, as all my criticisms were protected under freedom of speech human rights, I tweeted the following on 27 Apr 2023

"Latest on PCC Steve Turner's attempts to intimidate and silence his critics: he asked his own police force to investigate me for 'harassment' but they have concluded nothing I have said on social media constitutes harassment."

"It seems highly unethical for a Police and Crime Commissioner to ask his own force to investigate a critic but with Cleveland Police and PCC Steve Turner nothing should surprise #LocalElections2023 #Conservatives"

"The word which crops up constantly from people who have dealings with Cleveland Police PCC Steve Turner is 'bully' Well, I won't be bullied and will continue to hold him and the Conservative Party to account.
#LocalElections2023"

"Unlike Cleveland Police PCC Steve Turner I'm not one for wasting police time, but the question of how he was rejected by @Conservatives as a PCC candidate, then mysteriously

reinstated after an intervention by @SimonClarkeMP surely deserves a look?"

When I took the call from Cleveland Police to notify me of Turner's complaint, I was sitting by my mother-in-law's bedside in a palliative care ward of Whitehaven hospital in Cumbria. She sadly died a couple of days later from heart failure.

Now of course, neither Turner, nor Cleveland Police, had any idea of what my partner and I were going through at that time. But it's a serious reminder that when politicians can't take criticism, and seek to use the police to silence their critics, real people's lives get further disrupted and damaged. The pain they are already suffering is worsened. My experience of this is far less than others who have truly suffered at the hands of touchy politicians seeking to silence critics and I detail that elsewhere, but the point is true enough here too.

The fact I was seldom at home during this time, because of supporting my partner through his mother's terminal illness, either in Middlesbrough or across the country in Cumbria, is also relevant to the police investigation instigated by Turner. I believe my enforced absence spared me from a knock at the door and a raid by Cleveland Police.

I suspect the investigating officers called to discuss Turner's complaint, but I wasn't at home. My grounds for this are that others subjected to complaints by Turner *were* raided by the investigating officers, and the phone call I eventually took came from a sergeant based at the small police station in Loftus, where I usually live. Why give the case to that station unless they were planning to knock on my front door?

The next time Conservative politicians criticise the police for investigating 'hurty' comments on social media, remind them of the time one of their own PCCs did just that.

This was a waste of police time and resources if ever there was one. But worse than that also a disturbing misuse of police resources by the politician officially in charge of those resources. A chilling look into the police-state future some of those on the far-right of the Conservative Party would like to lead us towards. Especially if it silences criticism of them and the party.

By now I had also got wind of the much worse intimidation of local activists, including a hard working Conservative Party volunteer, and touched on it here, though much constrained by legal and welfare concerns:

"Conservative Party intimidation of critics locally has hit even worse lows than Cleveland Police and Crime Commissioner Steve Turner having me falsely investigated for 'harassment': others are suffering even worse.
I'll detail when I can."

On the issue of inappropriate use of sparse police resources:

"The next time @ClevelandPolice won't investigate your burglary, rest assured that they DO have time to investigate hurtful comments on social media about their PCC Steve Turner #LocalElections2023"

In response to incredulous replies about this on twitter:

"Oh, PCC Steve Turner definitely did raise a complaint against me with Cleveland Police. A police officer phoned me yesterday to say they'd considered it and my twitter comments came nowhere near harassment.

Funny how Tories usually bemoan police investigating hurt feelings"

By now I had also been made aware of the Cleveland Police *raids* on the homes of Turner's Labour Party opponent and their agent in the Longbeck Ward contest in the local elections:

"Disgraceful that PCC Steve Turner had officers from his own force doorstep political opponents over an election leaflet.
Looks like I got off lightly with a phone call.
Turner must resign and the Conservative Party should disown him"

They didn't, of course.

Following the Turner's eventual defeat in the last outstanding vote count of the 2023 local elections, the national media were now on the story, including tweets by Tom Larkin of Sky News

"One of the most remarkable tales of the local elections unfolded before a single vote was cast.

A story about power and democracy a long way from Westminster.

And this man - Steve Turner - who's the Conservative Police Commissioner for Redcar. He wanted a second job... THREAD

The thread went on to detail how an election leaflet put out by the Labour candidate, and quoting some of my criticisms of Steve Turner had led to a police investigation at Turner's behest, leading to police raids on the candidate and Labour activists' homes.

"Steve has been upset by your leaflet," an investigating officer was quoted as saying, in Kafkaesque fashion, during one of the raids.

Frankly, I was astonished at the turn of events and was contacted by Sam Coates, Deputy Political Editor of Sky News, to do an interview on it but was unfortunately sunning myself in Gran Canaria at the time and could only talk via Zoom.

Being thousands of miles away didn't stop me tweeting my reaction to events:

"So, three Labour activists visited by Cleveland Police, and I'm the fourth individual mentioned in the report, simply for criticism of PCC Steve Turner in a political campaign. What the hell has the Conservative Party become?"

The apparent basis for Turner calling in his own police force to investigate his political opponent, and critics such as myself, was his dislike of a leaflet put out by Luke Myers, his Labour opponent in the Longbeck Ward contest. This leaflet, in traditional Tory blue colours (a common 'trick' used by all political parties) had quoted my criticism, as the former Conservative Association Chairman, of Turner for standing for the role of councillor given his duties as PCC.

Every quote used was taken from social media and the local press, and Myers had previously contacted me to ask if he could quote me directly. I had declined to offer a direct quote to him, as I didn't want to be seen as endorsing anyone in the elections, but said that as far as I was concerned he was free to use any of my quotes already in the public sphere anyway.

It appears that Turner had alleged to Cleveland Police that the leaflets contained untruths about him as a candidate, contrary to Section 106 of the Representation of the People Act 1983.

As you'll read later on in the Chapter titled 'General Mayhem', I had some experience of defending a Tory candidate against a S106 accusation when I was Deputy Chairman Political at STCA, so I had been very careful to make sure none of my criticisms of Turner were in any way untrue. As Cleveland Police later rapidly concluded from their investigation.

But the spectacle of a police force raiding the political opponents of the local Conservative Police and Crime Commissioner had already been played out and caught the attention of the national media. A pretty shocking look into a troubling future if thin-skinned politicians are free to call in their own police forces to deal with criticism they don't like.

Turner, who is clearly developing a habit of complaining about criticism, went on to complain to Ofcom about Sky News' coverage of the affair. His complaint was dismissed, but did seemingly have a 'chilling' effect on further reports of goings on among Conservative politicians on Teesside. 'Chilling' in more ways than one, because I gave a further filmed interview to Sam Coates of Sky News, sat on a very cold and blustery Redcar seafront detailing my concerns, which was never broadcast, seemingly following Turner's complaint.

All the above should concern anybody, whatever their politics, who supports freedom of speech in a democracy, and crucially, the freedom to make honest, truthful criticisms of those in power. We neglect that freedom at our peril.

As an interesting postscript, and an example of just how toxic Conservative politics have become in their prized Tees Valley (and as evidence, in my defence, that I don't *always* disagree with the Turners) I offer one final tweet, commenting on the readmittance of former Conservative councillor Vera Rider to the party in November 2023. A former Conservative colleague of Turner's in Longbeck Ward, it's fair to say there's no love lost between them, and Turner had publicly expressed his opposition to the move:

"Shocked to be in agreement with Cleveland PCC Steve Turner, but the Conservative Party readmitting Cllr Vera Rider smacks of desperation. She was thrown out by the party as the most disruptive of local Tory Cllrs. Details in my book coming soon."

Chapter 6 - Ministerial Affairs or 'Falling Madly in Lust'

Since re-joining the Conservative Party in 2018, I had always enjoyed a good relationship with our local MP, Simon Clarke. In fact, it was his email response to my concerns about whether the party was truly committed to a fair deal for the North of England, the 'levelling-up agenda' as it became, that persuaded me that the party was once again worthy of support.

George Osborne, by contrast, with his 'Omnishambles' budget in 2012 and specifically his plans for regional pay and benefits, which would have stripped billions from the North and other English regions, had originally driven me out of the party.

Osborne seems to have a talent for offending people unnecessarily; his 'Project Fear' threats of a fiscal punishment-beating if people voted Leave in the EU Referendum were a case in point. The fact his regional pay plans never came to fruition and were quietly dropped as the dreadful idea they were (Liz Truss should have taken note before proposing and dropping a similar wheeze in 2022) made my 2012 resignation from the party, as a proud and offended Northerner, all the more galling and unnecessary. But such is life.

Under Theresa May however, and much more so under Boris Johnson, a fairer deal for the regions, what became known as 'Levelling Up', was very much central to Conservative Party policy. As it should be. Simon Clarke, as a newly elected MP for an historically marginal seat in the north of England had every reason to be both personally and politically committed to improving the economic wellbeing of his constituency and the whole Tees Valley region in which it sits.

Ironically, given his subsequent actions, Simon was one of the few Conservative beneficiaries of Theresa May's calamitous decision to call a snap general election in 2017, winning his seat from Labour as he did in that election. The previous Labour incumbent in Middlesbrough South and East Cleveland, Tom Blenkinsop, had stood down from parliament given his clear disagreements with Labour Leader Jeremy Corbyn and the direction of travel of the party under his leadership. Not having to face a generally popular and locally born incumbent no doubt helped Simon's cause in MSEC, as did the absence of Steve Turner as a Ukip rival.

Prime Minister Theresa May, to my mind, was an honourable and able politician with a genuinely strong sense of duty and public service. She had survived the usual ministerial graveyard of the Home Office for a considerable period of years, and had been acclaimed Conservative Leader following David Cameron's post-EUreferendum resignation, and the disintegration of the Boris Mark 1 leadership campaign in 2016.

May was not, however, a natural campaigner and the much derided 'Maybot' had lost the 22 seat majority inherited from Cameron, in the 2017 general election. Her subsequent dependence on Ulster Unionist support in Parliament and the increased power of hardline Brexiteer Tory MPs would haunt the rest of her premiership.

May's decision to call the election in 2017 was lambasted after the fact, but it has to be said that you'd have to be a saint to resist the temptation of doing so when the opinion polls regularly had you 20 points ahead of Corbyn's Labour, and you were faced with trying to drive through an extremely difficult Brexit with a narrow parliamentary majority.

Arguably, May's fault was not in calling the election when she did, but in the terrible campaign that followed. In addition to May's clunky campaign style, CCHQ had decided to fight an extremely expansive campaign, targeting seats which had been Labour for generations while arguably neglecting vulnerable Tory held seats (Stockton South under James Wharton being the perfect example of seats lost in that campaign.)

The Conservative Party's talent for fighting the wrong campaign at the wrong time is covered in another chapter, but put simply the 2017 campaign should have been fought in 2019, and vice versa. The party proved to be rather like the Mastermind contestant in the famous Two Ronnies sketch: confusingly but humorously answering the question before last.

May herself had also courageously, though as it turned out foolishly, decided to use her apparent massive lead in the opinion polls to propose a far-reaching, but politically challenging, solution to spiralling adult social care costs in the UK. Whilst these plans were generally fair to all concerned, not least the young workers being asked to fund care for the often wealthy elderly, they proved politically toxic.

The media dubbed them the 'dementia tax' or 'death tax' and the middle-aged kids of wealthy elderly parents took fright at the prospect of their inheritances being whittled down to £100,000 by their parents' care costs. Which begs the question of how much do these often well-off individuals insist upon inheriting? And how much do they expect today's (often hard-pressed) young taxpayers to pay to subsidise their inheritances? Generational fairness is something I'm a great believer in, but never having been likely to inherit a fortune anyway maybe makes that point of view a lot easier to hold.

But back to Simon Clarke, one of the few gainers from May's snap election as the newly elected MP for Middlesbrough South and East Cleveland. Simon was a former solicitor with a big London law firm, Slaughter and May (ironically enough, given the way he came to power in 2017) though his career in law seems to have taken a back seat to politics and a stint as a research assistant for, among others, Dominic Raab MP. But he does deserve credit for actually having some non-political career outside of parliament, unlike so many of our modern day career-politicians.

Simon was Middlesbrough born and bred, which no doubt helped his electoral chances over the usual Home Counties Tory candidates parachuted in by CCHQ. His refined accent, however, owed more to the local public school he had attended in Yarm than the tough backstreets of Middlesbrough. Or even its more pleasant southern suburbs which made up about half of Simon's new constituency.

By way of an aside, this perceived poshness was, quite perceptively, also suggested by no less than Andy Preston, one time independent Mayor of Middlesbrough, as one reason for Clarke's apparent dependence on his office manager and future Cleveland PCC Steve Turner. The theory recounted by Preston to me goes that posh boy and rather green new MP Clarke gained comfort from having a working class political bruiser such as Turner at his side. It's a solid theory I had never considered before my conversation with former mayor Preston, who deserves the credit for it.

As a committed Brexiteer Simon did however suit this strongly Leave voting area which combined the southern edge of Middlesbrough and the rural former pit villages and market towns of East Cleveland. That strong commitment to Brexit would prove troublesome for Theresa May, and potentially for Simon's hopes of quick advancement under her leadership. If it lasted.

On the personal front, Simon was married to Hannah with whom he had a young child, Edward. To all appearances they seemed a very happy young couple with an exciting future ahead of them, though Hannah did sometimes appear withdrawn and even vulnerable at times; shy and uncertain on the political and public scene.

On one occasion during the winter 2019 general election campaign, Hannah appeared at a canvassing session wrapped up like a little mouse against the cold sweeping in off the frigid North Sea. I distinctly, and fondly despite all that has happened since, recall Simon comforting her against both the physical cold and the political chill of the numerous Labour posters on show in the left-wing enclave in Saltburn by the Sea.

Hannah seemed genuinely concerned that her husband was about to lose his newly won seat and be thrown on the unemployment line, given the appearances of Labour posters and our reception in the town.

Thankfully for her, for Simon, and for us, the left-leaning, anti-brexit sentiments of central Saltburn folk were neither typical of the constituency nor the country as a whole. But on that grim, cold day in Saltburn's Sainsbury's car park, Simon cuddled and reassured Hannah that all was well, and he would win and keep his seat. It was a genuinely touching scene and spoke of the closeness between them. Politics can be a harsh business but there's a human dimension to it too which shouldn't be overlooked.

Depressingly, that affection and Hannah's unswerving support of her husband would be cruelly betrayed within a year.

For Simon would soon be embarking on a workplace affair with a junior civil servant that would lead to his divorce and resignation from government.

My first inkling of this drama came in a telephone call from Simon to me as his local association Chairman in September 2020.

I had been settling down to a quiet Sunday afternoon when my mobile rang and Simon's name came up. I imagined it would be a courtesy call about something trivial; a request for association funding for something or other, or for volunteer support for a planned campaign day. Instead Simon was calling to say that he had found himself under immense stress recently, both from the workload demanded as a minister for Levelling Up and Local Government and on the personal front.

He had tendered his resignation as a minister.

With this, I was stunned. Simon had appeared stressed and harassed lately and his workload both as a relatively new MP and junior minister was undoubtedly high and demanding, but I never expected this.

He added in the course of the conversation that he would be seeking a divorce from Hannah and the need to sort this and his new domestic arrangements out would also require much of his time, also necessitating his ministerial resignation.

Talk of divorce set alarm bells ringing and although I'm naturally squeamish about prying into people's private lives I allowed Simon to continue to talk and eventually guided him round to the reasons for the divorce. Simon admitted that he had grown close to a work colleague in the civil service, and whilst denying that the relationship had become physical at that point, he clearly hoped it would develop into something more, and that his marriage to Hannah was over.

Whilst I may be squeamish about prying into such matters I must say I found that assertion hard to believe, and suspect matters had progressed further and faster than Simon was letting on. But I'm also grown up enough to know that these things happen in life and especially, it seems, in politics. The story of an MP spending long weeks away from home at Westminster, apart from their wife and family, and falling for someone else when thrust into close working relationships with colleagues is a story as old as politics itself.

I'm no moralist, understand human frailty (I've plenty myself) and realise that the truth of what has happened in a relationship is really only known to the people in that relationship. As such I was inclined to go easy on Simon for this moral imperfection and as he really did seem shattered by recent events I was also concerned for his welfare. Even more so for Hannah, the wronged party in all this.

I told him that he had my continued support, that I understood these things happened and expressed my hope that he would take the time and space he needed to sort matters out and take care of his own mental health. I would also let the association executive know what had happened and would do my best to ensure their response was supportive and understanding also.

I was later told that Simon was surprised by how easy-going I was in response to all this. An MP losing his ministerial position, marriage and good name was something that in years gone by could have proved career ending.

It was certainly unwelcome news and yet another difficult matter for the association to deal with, especially as we became aware that The Sun newspaper had got wind of what was unfolding and was sniffing around the story. But as stated, I'm no bible bashing moralist and realistic about human relationships. I did later joke that

MPs on my watch get one affair and divorce, and one only. Any more than that and questions would be asked. Whilst intended humorously that probably wouldn't be far from the truth of my approach: these things happen in life and can be forgiven, but making a habit of it would be more problematic.

Later I prepared an email to my executive detailing the unwelcome news, emphasising just how much pressure Simon was under, how he needed to take time out to look after his mental health, and expressing the hope we would all be supportive of both him and Hannah in such difficult times. The response was overwhelmingly supportive and understanding, though the usual suspects among Simon's enemies in the local party responded accordingly. Cllr Philip Thomson, rather snidely to my mind, made a pointed remark about Simon's mental health and Cllr Vera Rider's reaction was all the more spiteful.

In an act of madness, and desperation at nobody else being willing to volunteer for the job, I had previously allowed Vera to input local *good news* stories from councillors onto the association's website. She contacted me soon after news of Simon's resignation to ask if she should put something on our website about it. I replied that it wasn't good news and 'least said soonest mended' and all that, so I didn't think we should. She persisted and suggested that local people would expect the association to say something, so I relented. I supplied her with a very supportive quote from me as Chairman expressing regret at what had happened but the association's strong continuing support for our hard working local MP, and said she could use that and just the basic fact of Simon's ministerial resignation for personal reasons.

The next day Vera had put a news item on Simon's resignation on our website without any mention of support from the association, let alone my quote.

It was typically vindictive of the councillor for Longbeck and I changed the website password, and removed her access privileges the same day. No doubt that was yet another perceived slight that added to her eventual walkout alongside the other disgruntled 'CIG' councillors (see the later chapter 'Councillors are revolting')

Very soon after Simon's resignation was made public, delayed by Boris being busy with something else (as usual) The Sun newspaper was back sniffing around for background on the story, apparently door stepping a tearful Hannah, and pursuing salacious local gossip.

The paper reported Simon as being 'head over heels in lust' with his new love and forced to resign his ministerial role in order to save her civil service job. (https://www.thesun.co.uk/news/12648544/married-tory-quit-cheating-wife/)

I've no idea where that quote came from, if it was genuine at all, but it wasn't from anybody locally at South Tees as far as I'm aware.

Luckily for Simon, in addition to societal attitudes to affairs becoming more liberal over time, the fact that 'Shagger' Johnson was Prime Minister and naturally disinclined to be moralistic about extramarital affairs would ensure that Simon's absence from government would not be a long one, and he would within months be promoted to cabinet level.

This favour in allowing a disgraced former minister back into government no doubt coloured Clarke's attitude to Johnson's own misdemeanours in public office, of which there were many, of course. For Simon would be an unswerving supporter of Boris to the very bitter end, excusing his many proven lies and other faults.

One gets the sense that those in public life who are willing to constantly excuse dishonesty on the part of others, such as Johnson, tend themselves to have a loose relationship with the truth and trustworthiness. My experience of Johnson supporters locally at South Tees rather confirms that impression. Mssrs Clarke, Turner and Houchen among them.

As for my own relationship with Simon Clarke, it's fair to say that Johnson's behaviour proved the final straw in an already deteriorating friendship.

When the infamous photo of Johnson raising a toast at a Downing Street leaving-party during lockdown was finally published, I commented on a whatsapp group we belonged to that it was proof that Johnson was indeed an habitual liar. Lies that would in due course see the buffoon thrown out of parliament.

Simon, of course, had me removed from the group almost immediately.

Chapter 7 - Drunken, Racist Violence

Shortly before he himself was suspended by the party in November 2019, and not long after the Conservative Councillor David Smith had been charged with child sex offences, our Chairman Malcolm

Griffiths cryptically alluded to yet another scandal about to break at South Tees Conservatives.

Leaving a typically fractious Executive Council meeting Malcolm remarked, almost casually, that the scandals we had been experiencing, and fretting about in the meeting that night, could well be about to be topped by one yet come to light. He would say no more than that and nobody was minded to press him on it. I wasn't on the best of terms with him at that point so felt doing so would be futile, as he wouldn't be inclined to tell me anyway. Other Executive members were on even worse terms, whilst those friendly to Malcolm probably didn't want to know in any case. The head-in-the-sand position might be a stupid one in the long term, but it's comforting for a short while.

I thought little more of the comment for several months, as we were all overtaken by events: firstly Boris calling his snap Brexit general election in November 2019 (which suspended normal association business anyhow), then Malcolm's own suspension by CCHQ and my sudden elevation to the Chairmanship. A poison chalice if ever there was one.

I took the view as acting Chairman that all other matters should be put aside as we concentrated 100% on winning the election, certainly in as much as retaining MSEC, and later by putting resources into Redcar as well, once the polling looked so favourable. Plus, as a one-off favour to the candidate, a little frigid, late-night canvassing in our (no-hope) Middlesbrough contest on one occasion.

All other matters were irrelevant until polling day had passed.

After the victory that resulted, and the celebrations that followed, we were quickly into Christmas, which proved a blessed relief from the all too often toxic nature of politics at STCA.

Come the new year of 2020 I was busy helping to find accommodation for Jacob Young's new constituency office in Redcar and getting Executive approval for loans and letting arrangements between Jacob and the association. Ironically this involved working closely with Steve Turner, who had now been appointed as Office Manager by Jacob as well as Simon Clarke.

However, the fallout from David Smith's downfall and his charging with child sex offences was about to come back, in a roundabout way, to haunt us, and resurrect Malcolm's cryptic warning.

Smith had been elected a Conservative councillor in Coulby Newham Ward on Middlesbrough Council the previous May, replacing the former Tory councillor there, the aforementioned Jacob Young MP. Smith, of course, really should never have been chosen to be a Conservative candidate at all, let alone one for an eminently winnable ward, and, as detailed earlier, it is alleged he did not go through the usual vetting or selection procedures.

This is a symptom of the Conservative's problem in the North East, and North generally, of struggling to find sufficient candidates to fight now winnable wards and even parliamentary seats. A party which for decades had been very much a minority in these parts, with few elected MPs or even local government officials, and a dwindling and ageing membership, was always going to struggle to find quality candidates given its new-found popularity after Brexit.

One allegation also has it that Smith was parachuted in to the ward at late notice mostly to spite an enemy of Malcolm in the local party who wanted the candidacy, but this an unconfirmed rumour, one among many in South Tees mythology.

Having originally refused to resign his council seat when charged with sex offences in June 2019, Smith was finally forced to do so after about six months due to his failure to attend any council meetings in that time. I understand he may have been in Ireland for part of that time, though that would seem odd given he was on bail for his alleged offences.

This would mean a council by-election in Coulby Newham, and although fighting one after the previous Tory councillor had resigned in such circumstances might not appear a very appetising prospect, we were still keen to contest it and field a strong candidate.
As luck would have it, our campaign manager had a very strong, local candidate in mind, someone who lived in the ward, had a compelling backstory, was very personable and a polished media performer. That candidate was Luke Mason, a young man who had campaigned for tougher sentencing for driving offences after he himself had been left for dead, and seriously injured, by a hit and run driver in Middlesbrough.

Although we had an ideal candidate, party rules still required us to advertise the vacancy to local members and I am nothing if not a stickler for the rules! And so, the vacancy was advertised and we requested expressions of interest from members qualified to stand in the Middlesbrough local government area.

A minor quandary arose when one application was received after the deadline, but from a member with disabilities: our campaign manager fretting that rejecting it at that stage would possibly bring a complaint under equalities legislation. I took the decision that if it was clear the application was late, and it was, we simply couldn't consider it and we should contact the applicant explaining as such and encouraging them to apply for future vacancies. Which we did without any hassle.

A much bigger quandary, in fact a huge potential quagmire, arose as we had got an application, unfortunately received before the deadline, from a member who had been the subject matter of Malcolm Griffith's cryptic warning about yet another brewing scandal at South Tees.

Our campaign manager, although aware, had failed to pass on the information Malcolm had been dealing with before his suspension, and Malcolm certainly didn't perform any kind of handover to me as his successor.

As it now turned out, one of our two applicants for the Coulby Newham vacancy had within the latter months of 2019 been the subject of complaints made to the association by members of the public alleging racist, drunken, and violent behaviour.

The fact this individual had previously also been the Conservative Party candidate for a very high profile position only made the matter far, far worse.

So, now muggings had been landed with the task of clearing up someone else's mess, as usual. By dealing with the application, the outstanding complaints, and hopefully avoiding yet more shit hitting the South Tees fan.

Our campaign manager worried about what to do with the application, as it, unlike the third one one received, had been valid under party rules. We didn't want to make the individual aware of the complaints at that stage but certainly didn't want to run the risk of ending up with them as our candidate. Even shortlisting and interviewing them would potentially bring the complaints to public attention, if they bragged about how they were going for another Tory candidacy.

Tell them they've failed the paper vetting sift, I suggested, and if they've got any complaints or queries to contact me. So we did, and they never queried it, as I suspect they knew what was in the offing re their alleged behaviour. As this was a by-election on a very short timescale we had more leeway (no pun intended) under party rules as to how we chose the candidate. I'm a stickler for rules, but sometimes circumstances dictate a little creativity with them is in order, especially where their vagueness permits.

And so South Tees Conservatives interviewed only one candidate for the vacancy and unanimously selected Luke Mason, the whole panel being impressed by the maturity and eloquence of a clearly very able young man, and helpfully somebody with no social media presence at all.

Who, incidentally, went on to win the by-election, held in the most dire of circumstances, by a country mile.

But what to do about the very troubling allegations against the unsuccessful applicant?

I managed to scrape together the original email complaints which had been forwarded from the association to Malcolm for him to deal with. Malcolm had acknowledged them, sympathised and promised action, but it had now been several months without anything at all being done on our part. Such was the malaise all too present at South Tees Conservatives.

From a moral point of view the allegations, if true, were appalling, such behaviour is simply unacceptable in any walk of life, let alone from somebody who aspires to be in public life.

From a political point of view, if publicised, they had the capacity to cause real damage to the party and its candidates in upcoming elections. At that stage they included not just the Coulby Newham by-election but the Tees Valley Mayoral and Cleveland PCC elections, which were due to be held (before covid intervened) in May 2020. The high profile contest that the individual had previously fought on behalf of the party would make the impact of the allegations all the more damaging.

It would also lay bare the altogether dangerously shoddy vetting and selection of candidates the party employs, which had already been highlighted by the David Smith experience.

I contacted the original complainant, apologised profusely for the lack of action and double checked that they still wanted to pursue the complaint, which they did. I arranged to meet with the complainants to assure them that I and the party took the matter seriously, to discuss further what had happened and to try to secure signed statements from them to use as evidence.

The alleged behaviour was truly appalling:

The complainants were drinkers in a local pub and acquaintances of the Conservative Party member who was also a pub regular It was a traditional, Teesside working-class bar, frequented mostly by men of working age and older, a pretty rough and ready place where banter could be quite hard-edged, and where customers aren't inclined to be easily offended.

It was clear that behaviour by our member, which had started off as being in the same vein, had recently become far more aggressive and offensive, culminating in a drunken, violent assault, motivated by racism.

Jokes about Meghan Markle's marriage into the Royal Family had culminated in the member asking if the Duke of Edinburgh would mind having a 'N-word' in the family. This caused particular offence to the complainant who had mixed race children in his own family, and culminated in a serious row.

The member also regularly mocked the complainants Irish heritage with jokes about IRA terrorists being a regular part of their 'repartee'.

It was clear that drink was a root cause of much of this behaviour. The individual was stated to be pleasant, and even funny, company when not in drink, but became increasingly aggressive, offensive and boorish the more they drank. This was confirmed by others I spoke to at the pub, not part of the complainant's group.

The misbehaviour culminated when, inebriated, the member had failed to negotiate a door, bumped into it and fallen over, causing laughter from those who witnessed it, much to the annoyance of the member concerned.

Later, they had drunkenly approached the complainant's father, a man in his 70s, at the entrance and tried to land a headbutt on the gentleman, but had fallen down themselves instead. They had later bragged to bar staff about planting a 'Glasgow kiss' on the individual. A pensioner.

This final misbehaviour had led to the member being permanently barred from the pub, something I was able to independently confirm.

I asked if the assault had been reported to the police, and if not why not, as failure to do so would cast doubt on the veracity of the complaint. The response was that his father was 'old school' and didn't want to involve the police in the matter, which seemed plausible enough. The complainant did however want there to be consequences for the attack and the other misbehaviour, and couldn't understand how the Conservative Party had ever selected such an individual for a high profile contest. Given the shoddy vetting employed by the party, I could however.

Having talked to the group, I was satisfied that the complaints were genuine and not motivated by a desire simply to cause political damage to the party. If anything, most of the group were sympathetic to the party, especially in the era of Brexit and Corbyn, and the complainant was partly motivated by a concern that the party should not suffer negative publicity as a result of the member's actions. If they had wanted to cause mischief for the party they would have gone public with the allegations, especially given the inaction by my predecessor. This was something I, naturally, was keen to avoid.

A sticking point was whether they were all willing to make signed statements confirming their allegations. Fear of reprisal from the member concerned, given their previous violent behaviour seemed a genuine concern that made them hesitate to put their names to the allegations as they would have to be disclosed to the member. I explained the disciplinary couldn't go ahead without them and I was very keen that the allegations should be considered by the party. After some reassurance I was able to persuade them to submit signed statements.

I also made further enquiries, of responsible and independent individuals, which corroborated all of the allegations, including the fact that the members' behaviour had led to a permanent barring from the premises. These sources weren't however willing to provide signed statements to that effect. I was satisfied, however, that the complaints were genuine, but would I be able to convince my Executive?

Liaising with regional staff in the 'professional' party, myself and what was left of the Association Officers of South Tees, following Malcolm and others's suspensions, determined that there was a genuine case to answer, and the member concerned was suspended pending further investigations and a likely expulsion hearing.

Suspension letters and emails were sent out.

The proforma suspension letter, whose use was dictated by the party nationally, was a typically shoddy piece of work by CCHQ. The form of words we had to use under party rules seemed to suggest that expulsion was a foregone conclusion even before the formal hearing of the Executive Council had taken place, at which the accused member would be allowed to respond to the allegations.

Crucially, this prompted an email from the accused member making precisely that point: what was the point of a hearing when the letter suggested they would be expelled anyway? I got our Membership Secretary to reply that we agreed and sympathised that the form of words was misleading, but to reassure them that the process wasn't a foregone conclusion. That they would get a chance to respond to the allegations and the Executive Council would only decide whether to expel them at that point, and on the basis of the evidence they had heard from both them and the complainant.

This email response was crucial because the member would later claim, from an entirely new email address, not to have received the email giving notice of the hearing date, which was sent to them at the email address we had on their membership record and from which they had replied to the initial suspension email. Either they had *genuinely* changed email addresses and not bothered to inform us, which would be lax on their part, especially in the middle of a disciplinary process, or, far more likely, they were playing silly buggers after the event.

For this whole process was about to be interrupted and upended by Covid 19. An original date for the hearing had been set and the charges and witness statements in support had been supplied to the 'accused' by post and email. As the whole country went into gradual restrictions, and then sudden lockdown, it became impossible to hold the disciplinary hearing on the given date or within the timescales prescribed by the party and, frustratingly, everything was placed on hold.

Several months later when the country finally began emerging from its covid cocoon and the party issued new covid guidance on carrying out disciplinary hearings on Zoom we had moved on to autumn 2020. The usual requirement of letters sent by recorded delivery was done away with in favour of emails only, which handily could contain the hyperlinks to log into the meetings. The member concerned was informed by email of the date and time of the hearing and sent the link. Reminders also were sent. But on the night in question the accused simply wasn't there.

This was disappointing, as although under party rules we could proceed with the case anyway in the member's absence, it strangely enough weakened the case against them. I wanted to be able to put various accusations to the member directly, and to try to trip them up with their responses. In particular I wanted to ask them if they *were* barred from the pub in question, something asserted by the complainants, and verified independently to me, but crucially off the record.

If they accepted they had been barred it would beg the question why? Struggling pubs don't bar good customers for the fun of it after all.

If they denied being barred altogether I would have offered to reconvene the hearing at the pub to test this, or at the very least phoned the pub there and then during the hearing to ask about the member's status. I knew for a fact the member had been barred and for the reasons stated, but might struggle to prove this in their absence,

So paradoxically, the member's failure to attend weakened the case and after presenting it and taking questions on it from the panel I was alarmed that there seemed scepticism about the claims from some members of the executive, or that somehow the complained-of behaviour didn't warrant suspension. This may be a cultural thing, an age thing, as most of the Executive were older and perhaps more relaxed at accusations of racism, or mere 'banter', than they should have been.

Sensing the 'room', and faced with the danger that this individual would escape suspension, with all the negative repercussions that entailed, I stuck my neck out and put my reputation on the line.

I had, I confirmed, made further enquiries of independent witnesses who had corroborated all the allegations of the complainants. I had no doubts on that basis of the truth of the complaints. I couldn't disclose the nature of those further enquiries due to assurances given, but if the panel had doubts as to what they were, they might consider what further enquiries they would have made in my position. And that if the panel regarded me as honest and trustworthy, they should have no doubt as to the veracity of the allegations levelled at the member concerned.

I was perhaps sailing close to the wind in this. It wouldn't stand up in a criminal court of law, hearsay rules and all that, but based on the rules of the Conservative Party and natural justice I felt I was doing the right thing, and still do.

I can't stand racists or drunken thugs, and if justice requires a little helping hand to overcome barriers created by fear of intimidation, then so be it.

The panel found unanimously for expulsion.

As the accused had not turned up at the meeting on Zoom, and as they had a final right of appeal to CCHQ, I sent confirmation of their expulsion by both email and letter, a belt and braces approach, not actually required under the party's Covid disciplinary rules.

And, lo and behold, a few days later the member concerned sent an email from an entirely new email address claiming they had never received the email notice of the hearing or the zoom link at all. Playing silly buggers was clearly something they enjoyed.

I replied that if that was *really* the case, they had an automatic right of appeal to the Conservative Party nationally anyway, and then advised them of the time limits and the named individual and address that they should send their appeal to.

No appeal was ever forthcoming, of course.

The whole episode exposed just how shoddy Conservative Party vetting of candidates locally can be. In other chapters I detail how bad the vetting and selection of candidates can be nationally.

The state of the country today is evidence of just how bad selection of candidates can be, and the problems that result. Our country deserves better.

The Conservative Party may well be a victim of its own success in recent years, of suddenly becoming competitive in places like the North of England, where for decades they have merely been also-rans. It is some excuse, but that shoddy approach to choosing candidates presents very real dangers to those affected by some of the wholly unsuitable individuals placed in positions of power. The vulnerable, and society as a whole, suffer as a result.

The only upside in all this is that given the state of the party now in early 2024, I suspect this danger is about to be permanently removed. That can only be a good thing, but voters in this part of the world do deserve a genuine and viable alternative to the one-party Labour rule that previously applied.

I only hope that that alternative can emerge from the chaos to come.

Chapter 8 - Boris, Buffoonery, Brexit and Ben

I have a confession to make.

I voted for Boris Johnson to become Conservative Party leader, and therefore Prime Minister, in the Conservative Party leadership election in summer 2019.

There, 'tis done.

For all my later falling foul of party discipline for a forgotten tweet dating from 2018, where I stated in full unforgiving black and white pixels that I felt that Boris Johnson was a 'buffoon', I actually did vote for him to become leader the following year.

In my defence, given the shambles that followed, my view was that Johnson was the right buffoon for the job at that moment in time.

And arguably better than Jeremy Hunt.

For I took the view that both the Conservative Party and the country were in such a god awful mess due to the impasse over brexit, the paralysis inflicted on virtually every other pressing matter by the inability to put into action the result of the 2016 referendum, that both required shock treatment to resolve the appalling psycho-drama and force a conclusion. One way or another. Such was the very real damage being inflicted upon our society by the toxic inertia that prevailed at the time.

Boris Johnson, for all his manifold faults, his habitual dishonesty, and my (if I might say so) astutely spotted buffoonery, WAS that shock treatment.

I also took the view that he, and he overwhelmingly, was the paramount cause of the mess we were in, and therefore he should be tasked to clear it up. Or face the ignominy of being seen to fail spectacularly to do so.

The alternative in the final vote of party members for the leadership in summer 2019 was Jeremy Hunt. I took the view that Hunt would simply, and disastrously, be 'continuity May' and would likewise be unable to take the actions necessary to drive through a resolution to the Brexit impasse crippling government.

In a mess as complex as that created by the victorious Leave vote in 2016, on a false prospectus offered by Johnson, Gove and Co (remember how shell shocked they looked when they actually won?)

it probably required an unprincipled charlatan like Johnson to push a resolution through. Or to kill the whole project by proving that what they promised was actually undeliverable.

Resolution, one way or another, was what the party and the country needed by late 2019.

At the hustings held at the Hippodrome Theatre in Darlington during the contest, Hunt's performance served to confirm my fears about him as a potential party leader and PM. He was awkward, stilted and appeared a little flaky at times.

In response to one question he referred to the holocaust as a 'stain on Britain's history', which was either an example of a lack of historical knowledge or a propensity to mis-speak. The holocaust is a stain on humanity and human history, but given the 'blood and gold' Britain expended in defeating the Nazis, the actual architects and perpetrators of the holocaust, it's odd to regard it as a 'stain on British history'. (Britain has many shameful episodes in its history, alongside many glorious and laudable ones, just like any other country in the world, but the holocaust is not one of them) And 'odd' was a good description of Hunt all round: slightly tense, slightly shifty looking, awkward, and certainly not the ebullient campaigner we all knew Boris to be.

So, reluctantly and with plenty of misgivings I took a 'Back Boris' badge from the true believers like Jacob Young and Steve Turner at the event and plumped for Boris, an entirely flawed individual, but someone slightly less flawed perhaps than the alternative.

One of my colleagues on the STCA Executive, who proved a far better political oracle than I ever will be, addressed my reticence about Boris by saying that yes, in all likelihood he would implode spectacularly within a couple of years, but that he might just do some good in the meantime. And so it proved. Although the self-same colleague later blotted their copybook and reputation as a political seer by backing Truss in 2022. He clearly didn't see THAT coming.

Finally, (in my defence) I took the view that given all the above, Johnson was probably best placed to defeat Labour leader Jeremy Corbyn in an election that looked increasingly likely. For Corbyn, in my view, then as now, would have been an even greater catastrophe for this country than Boris possibly could be, and actually proved. Many times over.

Corbyn's far-left, pro-Russian, pro-terrorist, pro-pacifist, neo-marxist views of the world may undoubtedly be sincerely held, his supporters speak highly of how honest and decent he is in person, but they would have been a disaster for Britain. Between Boris' dishonesty and buffoonery and Corbyn's extremism, it was Corbyn who was the clear and present danger facing Britain, in my opinion.

Internationally, his sympathies for terrorist regimes and groups, including Putin's Russia (remember his reticence in condemning the murder of a British citizen and the nerve-agent poisoning of others in Salisbury by Putin's goons) would have been disastrous for our country's national security and our international alliances. I shudder to think what a Corbyn-led Britain's response to the invasion of Ukraine by Putin's gangster-fascist regime would have been. For that was one call that Johnson, to his credit, got right.

Domestically, his old school socialist approach would have led to massive spending, higher borrowing, higher taxation for all (as the rich picked up their wealth and fled), and the gross inefficiency that always goes hand in hand with socialist economics and systems of government.

A good example of how voters saw through the Corbyn offer during the 2019 election was the Labour Party's proposal to give everybody free broadband provided by the state. Ordinary people in the wilds of East Cleveland didn't buy it: they knew free stuff is generally poor quality. It would have crowded out private provision from the market (a market that actually is one of the few that is competitive and that works well in the UK. (Thank you TalkTalk for my £130 Tesco gift card for staying with you on a cheaper deal; shop around and threaten to change provider, folks!) A state-run free broadband killing private competition and all for a likely diet of Cuban dance collectives and Venezuelan knitting circles courtesy of Comrade Corbyn. Thanks, but no thanks, said the voters.

As such Boris, with his undoubted showmanship, raffish charisma and 'Get Brexit Done' message seemed best placed to defeat the very real threat that was Corbyn. And so it proved.

Boris *is* an entertainer. He *is* at times undeniably likeable. Buffoons often are.

He is an adept campaigner with an undoubted appeal to a certain section of the community. Some people DO actually like the *'bluster, bluster, piffle, piffle, ruffle hair, repeat'* schtick that Boris does so well.

This is true of voters generally, as the 2019 election proved, but also especially true of many Conservative Party members (though he is of course also a marmite type character who almost as many loathe as love, within the party as well)

With regard to the voters I spoke to in the winter election of 2019, there was genuine affection and support for Johnson among some. Though his impact on the election, certainly in Middlesbrough South and East Cleveland, was dwarfed by the far greater factors of delivering Brexit (in an overwhelmingly Leave voting region) and a deep seated animosity to Jeremy Corbyn, most notably among lifelong Labour voters. These two things were the dominant factors in delivering the Conservative Party and Johnson the 80 seat majority they have so spectacularly squandered since.

Johnsonites, most noticeably Simon Clarke, Ben Houchen and their ilk, love to overstate the importance of the Boris factor in the victory in 2019. It has been a central plank in their defence of Johnson's dishonesty and chaos ever since. Both in seeking to prevent his overthrow following the partygate scandals and 'Pincher by name, Pincher by nature' affair in 2022, and in their failed attempts to re-crown their 'king over the water' since (Boris being over the water mostly on the lucrative US speaking tour.) In doing so, they have parroted that 'Boris won us the 2019 election'

In my personal experience, as detailed above, this isn't really true. The Tories owed more to Jeremy Corbyn for their victory in 2019 than they did Boris Johnson, but that's no argument for making Corbyn Tory leader either.

Within the party itself I would say a clear majority of members truly love Boris. A much smaller group hate him, and those in between do have the 'transactional' approach shared by most Tory MPs: in as much as they loved him when he was an electoral asset, but that love is not blind to his many, many flaws (unlike the Clarkes, Dorries and Jenkins of this world) As such, when the flaws outweighed the asset value in electoral terms, Johnson was out of the window. Along with his wallpaper.

Examples of the genuine affection among party members for Boris Johnson are numerous. Locally, members were falling over themselves to fork out £70 each to attend a dinner with the 'great man' at Sir John Hall's Wynyard estate, and this was before Johnson had even become party leader and Prime Minister. Photos with the blond bombshell appeared everywhere on member's social media accounts locally, such was the popularity of the man and desire to be seen with him. I'm not sure whether photos were charged for, but knowing Johnson and his voracious appetite for money, I wouldn't be surprised if they were.

My absence was noted by some of those who were there, which I explained away as the £70 price tag being a little too steep for a tight-fisted Yorkshireman such as myself. This was mostly true, I didn't have any great animosity for Johnson at that stage but the actual ambivalence I did have didn't stretch to two tickets at 140 quid, plus associated travel and refreshment costs.

Another example of what I would regard as blind affection for Boris Johnson among the party membership occurred at Party Conference in 2021. Long queues formed early in the morning on the final day for the leader's speech, snaking back and forth among the stalls and stands in the cavernous hall of the GMEX Centre. Covid restrictions had largely been lifted by then and the numbers attending were huge compared to covid era events. So much so that an entirely separate arena had been secretly prepared for the great one's speech, unveiled at the last minute to great acclaim.

Not being willing to stand in line all morning, and with an eye to making a swift getaway home afterwards, I ended up filing into an overflow auditorium to watch the speech on a live video link and big screen. Two rows in front of me came to sit two stereotypical 'Tory Boy' types in tweedy suits, seated precisely with briefcases and umbrellas (this was Manchester afterall) stashed carefully to one side.

Throughout Boris' largely underwhelming speech, his vaudeville act really having worn very thin with me by then, these two characters billed and cooed adoringly. Occasionally they would repeat back to one another some of Johnson's pretty hackneyed phrases, like some kind of well-to-do Beavis and Butthead clones. Now, these two characters were probably in their teens or early twenties and so could be forgiven their adoring naivety, but how then do we explain the much older adoring fan base that Johnson still holds within party ranks?

Some are out and out Brexiteers, formerly ukippers, for whom Johnson will always be a garlanded hero of old for having delivered their longed for 'freedom from EU 'tyranny'. To them Boris could do no wrong, in the past, the present and forward into an endless future of adoration.

Others seem taken in by the posh boy, old Etonian, plummy voiced persona of Johnson: class snobbery still being highly prevalent within the party. A posh voice booming out seemingly clever platitudes, liberally throwing in obscure classical references from an Oxbridge education, does seem to get the juices flowing with this crowd. Add in an occasionally bumbling delivery, rakish glint in the eye and endearing ruffle of the blond mop and the affection is secured.

Others are simply grateful for the victory delivered in 2019, and a landslide hardly even dreamt of since the days of Thatcher. This was indeed a (largely) unexpected triumph, though yet again the adoration of the Boris fans tends to overlook the fact that in that 'BBC election' (Brexit, Boris and Corbyn) Boris was the least of the three factors that guaranteed a Tory victory. That's not my undoubted dislike of the man coming through but merely what I picked up from speaking to countless voters on umpteen doorsteps during the campaign.

Johnson is aided in his popularity by his uncanny additional ability to appear as all things to all men. To those on the hard right of the party he's the hard right deliverer of Brexit freedoms and low-spend, low taxation Conservative purity (if only the wicked Sunak would let him.)

To others he's a classical liberal, whose time as London Mayor showed to be far more enlightened on matters such as immigration and social liberalism.

In truth I'm not sure which of these things Johnson is, and I'm not sure he is either. His writing of both a pro and anti brexit piece prior to coming out for Leave being possibly the perfect example of this.

At heart, as his Eton school reports make out, Johnson is really all about Johnson. He's intrinsically self-absorbed, in public life for himself and what he can get out of it, and he can meld his principles accordingly. The chaos that ensued in his government is partly a testament to his own chaotic personality, his desire to please everybody and be all things to all men, and his lack of any strong underpinning beliefs and principles.

Add to that a clear obsession with trying to carve out a Churchillian legacy in British history, from an individual lacking any of Churchill's extraordinary talents, and the pen portrait is complete. Despite the unquestioning adoration of so many of his admirers, which has actually done so much damage to the Conservative Party as a cohesive force, Johnson is at best a Poundshop Churchill. Though that is probably an insult both to Churchill and to Poundshops.

I like to think it's my awareness of all this that seems to place me among the minority of Tories immune to Johnson's charms. Maybe that makes me sound a little smug and self-satisfied, if so, guilty as charged!

As stated above, I recognised his value in delivering Brexit and an election victory in very difficult circumstances. I recognise his showmanship, charisma and election winning campaign skills.

But I abhor the chaos that follows him around and the resulting egregious dishonesty he deploys, with such ease, to cover up that chaos inherent in his character. Boris' lack of preparation and mastery of his brief may seem entertainingly haphazard in after-dinner speaking but when pressed on actual detail on serious matters he tends to just make stuff up to get himself off the hook. And in government that proves fatal, eventually.

As much as some voters may enjoy the pantomime that Johnson brings to public life, the knock-about humour, rakish ways and 'anything is possible' 'boosterism', the sobering reality is that running a country of some nearly 70 million people is not like being the clown in a three ring circus. It's a deadly serious business, and the fact that Johnson's government ended up looking just like a circus is condemnation enough.

As Boris has shown, succeeding in politics is easy if you're prepared to make stuff up and tell outright lies when necessary, but eventually it catches up with you, and the damage done in the meantime can be immense. The dreadful state of the UK currently, and of the Conservative Party for that matter, has numerous causes, but prominent among them has been the chaotic misgovernment of both by Johnson and his acolytes.

It would no doubt be pointed out by his admirers that he was dealt a tough hand by Covid 19, which both disrupted the UK moving forward and dealing with the new reality and possible opportunities of Brexit, and placed a huge demand on government time and resources whilst hamstringing its ability to act. This is true, to an extent: the pandemic would have challenged the most able of Prime Ministers and the most efficient of governments, which simply weren't there under Boris' chaotic leadership. But even here Boris' character flaws made a bad situation worse, and that is almost unforgivable.

In voting for Boris as party leader in 2019 I had hoped (naively as it turned out) that when finally elevated to the highest office he had so clearly coveted his whole life (stating famously he wanted to be 'World King' at a very tender age) he would buckle down and apply himself to the job. That the enormity and importance of the role would bring out the serious side of his nature (if it exists) and promote the incredible intelligence his admirers are so keen to proclaim he possesses (not something I've ever noticed, sadly. Chucking a bit of schoolboy latin into conversation is not actually a genuine indicator of IQ)

Rather than bringing out such qualities, in the gravest crisis the UK had faced since the war, Covid instead served only to highlight the glaring failings in Boris' character.

The lack of a grasp of detail and mastery of a brief has been highlighted by the Covid inquiry, where various government scientists have opined that Boris appeared to struggle to even understand the basic science of the pandemic.

The flip-flopping on crucial decisions caused by his lack of decisiveness and underpinning principles.

Likewise the chaotic decision making that resulted from running an administration where no one person seemed to be in charge and instead 'court favourites' such as his wife or Dominic Cummings vied for favour.

The 'boosterism' of unjustified optimism that saw him reluctant to impose restrictions as early as they might have been, and that led to mixed messaging from the very outset.

The desire to be liked, that also made him reluctant to impose restrictions felt necessary on the basis of the scientific advice, and likewise meant that he failed to enforce those restrictions under his own roof at 10 Downing Street.

And the final, and as it proved, fatal flaw; as he reverted to his default setting of telling lies when cornered by difficult questions over covid rule breaking parties at number 10.

This, of course, eventually after a long drawn out process that further damaged the Conservative Party's reputation, saw him suspended from the House of Commons and prompted his resignation as an MP, in fear of a recall petition leading to a contest in his constituency that would in all likelihood see him thrown out.

All the covid rule breaking by Johnson himself and by his own staff on his watch, and the lies he told to cover them up, hit home on a personal level given the sacrifices I, my family and so many others had made to comply with the (often idiotic) rules imposed by government to try to suppress the disease.

In particular, I was forced to move out of my own home for the duration of the first lockdown, about three months in all, to move in with my partner, otherwise we would have been legally prevented from seeing one another for the duration. This being despite the fact that we each lived alone in our own homes and so the danger of transmitting the disease to others in our respective households was actually non-existent. If you discount my partner's cats.

The thought of being legally barred from seeing my partner of 20 plus years was made much worse by the fact my partner, working in the NHS, was on the very front line of the fight against covid, and so was at higher risk of contracting the disease. There was no way I was going to let my partner face that danger alone and unsupported, and so in the first week of lockdown I locked up my own house, filled a couple of holdalls full of clothes and moved to Middlesbrough to be with my partner for the duration.

Back then of course, in the early days of the pandemic nobody was entirely sure just how deadly the disease was, or just what the future would hold. With hindsight we have probably forgotten the dread the disease inspired at the time and thoughts of illness and death were all around. Grim times, but we were determined to face them together and to support one another through them.

The fact my partner spent much of the first lockdown doing gruelling 12 hour shifts in full PPE administering chest x-rays to patients dying from covid was some of the nightmare I was determined to support them through. We suffered less than many who lost loved ones, thankfully, but the experience does make one less inclined to forgive Johnson and team's contemptuous behaviour in Number 10.

The aforementioned idiotic nature of some of the rules became even clearer as restrictions eased and there came a point where I was legally entitled to travel to the street where my own home was situated, walk up and down it to my heart's content, even sit on my front patio and have a picnic if I chose, but would be breaking the law if I put my own key in my own front door and entered my own, empty, home. The fact my home is a very old, pretty ramshackle stone cottage in one of the more deprived bits of East Cleveland didn't make my legally enforced absence any easier to tolerate, given the worry of what was actually going on while I was away.

Given all the above, you might understand why Boris and Co's Downing Street rule breaking proved particularly offensive to me, among the millions of others who suffered far worse.

When details of partying at the heart of government emerged it both angered me and confirmed my worst fears about the kind of administration Johnson was running, and the fatal character flaws that underpinned it.

When the notorious photo of Johnson finally emerged, wine glass raised in a toast to those present at a Downing Street leaving do, stood before a table groaning with booze, I commented in the whatsapp group that included Simon Clarke that this proved that Johnson's denials of partying at number 10 before the House of Commons were indeed lies and that he was indeed the habitual liar he was so often accused of being. Simon did not respond in defence of his hero, which says something about Simon's character as well.

Of course Johnson's demise in early summer 2022 was not directly the result of covid, partygate or his telling lies at the despatch box of the House of Commons. It was 'Pinchergate' that finally did for him, and the fact government MPs and ministers had finally tired of being sent out before the media to repeat Johnson's untruths.

The fact that Johnson had promoted Chris 'Pincher by name, pincher by nature' (Johnson's own words apparently) Pincher to the Whip's Office and put him in charge of MP's discipline, whilst knowing from his time as Foreign Secretary that Pincher had been the subject of at least one complaint of sexual harassment was bad enough.

The fact Johnson's denial of this knowledge was then comprehensively rebutted by the former head of the Foreign Office civil service and proven to be yet another lie was the final straw. The much maligned civil service can at least still serve one of its functions of trying to keep its political masters honest.

I ventured the opinion that this extra revelation of dishonesty was probably the deserved end of Johnson on Nicky Campbell's Radio 5 talk show but even then I was probably, and depressingly, still in a minority among Conservatives in wanting to see Johnson gone. You simply cannot have a Prime Minister whose default setting in a tight spot is to tell blatant lies, both on grounds or morality (which still matters in my opinion in politics) and on grounds of practical government. Ministers need to have some certainty, even now after years of spin, half-truths and downright lies that when they repeat the party line it is fundamentally true.

Thankfully a majority of Tory MPs did feel the same way as me, as mass resignations followed and Johnson was left struggling even to fill the role of office tea boy with anybody willing to serve under him.

If there was any comfort in all this it is that the events of Johnson's time in power and his downfall confirmed my original judgement of him that he was a buffoon.

For way back in 2018, before I was actively involved in the party, and while Johnson was disgracing himself as a backbencher (with such lucrative and illuminating opinion pieces on police investigations into historic sex abuse: money 'spaffed up the wall' in Johnsons view, and burkas: 'letterboxes', 'bank-robbers' etc) I tweeted in response to someone accusing me of being a Boris fanboy (oh the irony) that I actually thought he was a buffoon.

My judgement on that at least was sound.

The fact that that very tweet got me barred from the party's candidates list in 2022 and subsequently prompted my leaving the

Boris Johnson led party could be viewed as a slightly worse case of judgement on my part. I agree that saying such unkind things about potential future party leaders isn't very diplomatic, nor good politics for that matter, if you may end up a candidate under such a leader. Such honest, northern plain speaking may be valued in these parts, and arguably British politics is crying out for it, but clearly it isn't favoured at CCHQ.

However, given that it led to me not having to try to defend the utter shambles the Conservatives have foisted on the British people ever since, and it's freed me up to shine a light on the true nature of the Conservative party in this book, I'd say it's been a good thing.

Ben

Tees Valley Mayor Ben Houchen's fortunes are in many ways closely linked to those of Boris Johnson himself. Although not possessing the ebullient showmanship of Johnson, Houchen has shown himself to be an astute politician, and through good fortune became very much the poster boy of Johnsons' much promoted 'Levelling up' agenda.

The fact that in financial terms and actual results that agenda has proved as illusory as many other Johnson promises has not (yet) damaged Houchen, as Teesside has undoubtedly been the main beneficiary of what Levelling Up spending there has been.

That much of that spending, so far at least, appears to have benefitted a small group of local businessmen, in return for minimal financial risk and input themselves, and at the expense of taxpayers and good governance, may (yet) prove Ben's undoing.

Personally, I always found Ben Houchen to be a pleasant individual, who genuinely means well for the local area, his home turf. On the downside, Ben is not universally liked even in Tory circles, has a tendency to be distant and hard to pin down at times, to over-promise and underdeliver. He is clearly also not as astute a businessman as his own publicity machine would like to make out.

Houchen's slavish support for Boris Johnson, his political benefactor, right up to and beyond the bitter end of Johnson's chaotic premiership is also undoubtedly a black mark against Houchen's judgement (among other Teesside MPs.) One might charitably put this down to Ben's obvious self-interest in trying to ensure that the 'Levelling Up' funding kept flowing under Boris' stewardship. But to my mind, a willingness to excuse habitual dishonesty on the part of others, so common among the Johnsonites, must call into question the commitment to the truth of the apologists themselves.

Whether the lack of adequate oversight, financial control and value for money at the 'Teesworks' development, highlighted by the recent government report (https://www.gov.uk/government/publications/independent-review-report-south-tees-development-corporation-and-teesworks-joint-venture/independent-review-report-south-tees-development-corporation-and-teesworks-joint-venture-executive-summary-and-recommendations) hides anything more sinister is beyond the scope of this book, my investigative powers and the currently available facts. Many other far more dedicated investigative journalists and activists have covered these issues in far more depth and I heartily recommend their efforts.

The most charitable reading of the report, to my mind, was that Ben (and hence taxpayers) appear to have been fleeced by far more commercially astute businessmen, who currently appear to be the main beneficiaries of the 100s of millions of pounds of public funds sunk into the project.

A lack of commercial nous and hard-headed public interest, and in its place some rather obvious naivety, currently at least, seems to be the worst misbehaviour at Teesworks and the South Tees

Development Corporation. Combined perhaps with an overbearing political self-interest in wanting to see rapid progress being made at an unacceptably high, and unjust, public cost. This in itself would represent a serious failing by a senior public figure, and the whole structure, arrangements and transactions around the Teesworks site should now be subjected to a full National Audit Office investigation if public confidence is to be restored.

The political element mentioned above is particularly relevant as there is no doubt that Ben Houchen *is* politically astute.

After a surprise victory over his Labour opponent in the Tees Valley Mayoral election in 2017, won on second preference votes, Houchen set about his task as Mayor with populist and politically-clever gusto. The economics of some of the decisions taken is, however, more questionable.

Durham/Tees Valley Airport was saved from potential closure and brought into public ownership by Houchen, in a move more befitting old-style socialist state intervention, that had some on the Tory right locally spluttering into their G and Ts. In a further populist move it was renamed to 'Teesside International Airport' after public consultation.

The fact that at the time any flights, let alone international ones, were thin on the ground at an airport with few routes at all, didn't seem to matter. This was a populist vote of confidence in the economic future of the region which still carries considerable public support locally.

That this public ownership came just before Covid grounded so much international air travel was perhaps the only bad luck that Houchen has suffered in his time as Mayor, necessitating as it did many tens of millions of pounds in public support for an airport now even emptier than before.

But as air travel recovered and extra routes were added, politically astute Ben was ever present at the foot of the aeroplane steps to welcome aboard travellers like some beaming, slightly overweight trolley-dolly. All for the cameras, of course, and the extensive publicity fund well used by this media-aware politician.

As mentioned above, Ben is not universally liked by local Conservatives, and one particular incident in my time as Chairman at South Tees sent relations into an even deeper deep-freeze, but again, is evidence of Houchen's political nous.

The issue was free school meals during covid lockdowns and summer holidays, and the Johnson government, and in turn local Tory MPs like Simon Clarke and Jacob Young had set their nose against extra support for hard pressed families in the form of extra free school meals out of term-time.

Now there *is* a legitimate debate to be had about the relative responsibilities of parents and the state in supporting children, especially on fundamentals like food, but the time for that debate is NOT during a global pandemic and massive economic insecurity, when just about all parents are fearing for their ability to put food on the table.

Ben saw that, I saw that, but sadly initially at least (before the habitual screeching u-turn) the Johnson government, and its hangers-on, didn't see that.

When Ben publicly came out in support of extra free school meals against the party line, and no doubt with one eye on his upcoming re-election campaign in a hard-pressed Teesside, others in the party were apoplectic. Some local MPs and some councillors in particular were especially upset and it took some effort to calm them down and persuade them that Ben's re-election was important to their survival too, and his actions were politically, on Teesside at least, entirely the right thing to do.

The inevitable u-turn when it came simply confirmed the Johnson government's chaos, lack of resolve and political acuity. And confirmed Ben Houchen's political judgement and popularity, reinforced by his landslide election victory in May 2021.

It is a sign of how far the Tory party's fortunes have fallen since then that Ben Houchen, once strongly rumoured to have been looking for a safe Conservative parliamentary seat, instead took ermine in Johnson's resignation honours. Now Lord Ben has one of the few safe Tory seats left, in the House of Lords, in a country where even true blue Rishi country of Richmondshire is, on some polling at least, under threat from Labour.

Whether Lord Houchen retains the Tees Valley mayoralty remains to be seen, as does the effect of having to deal with a likely Labour government in London far less generous, and forgiving, than that of Houchen's hero, Boris.

Chapter 9 - Dangerous Cosplay

I had never had a very high opinion of Liz Truss during her almost imperceptible rise through the ranks of Tory MPs and ministers. She appeared a bit vague, distant, and hard-to-place most of the time. Limited even.

That said, her approach to being Foreign Secretary, which was to treat the role as one long photoshoot for instagram, official photographer included, certainly raised her public image. Though not necessarily in a good way.

I'd seen the 'pork markets' and 'cheese-disgrace' speech she gave as a Trade Minister at a party conference on Youtube, and it was in equal measures amusing and alarming. How *does* somebody so lacking in self awareness, let alone public speaking ability, get to be a Cabinet minister? What does that alone tell us about modern politics, and the Conservative Party in particular?

So, by the Tory Conference in 2021 I had limited expectations when Liz popped up as Foreign Secretary to deliver an impromptu speech at a reception I was attending. But much to my surprise, she actually impressed me. Possibly for the first, and last, time.

It may have been the free glasses of Australian sparkling wine that myself and my companions from South Tees were quaffing that improved (or worsened, depending which way you look at it) my perception of Liz Truss' speech.

It may have been the euphoria that by pure good luck (and our intended reception being full) we were gatecrashing a *very good* reception by the Conservative Friends of Australia. For we had forgone a potentially quite dull round-table discussion on some obscure policy issue (the free food included being the main attraction, for it was tea-time) for this last minute alternative. Which offered the even better attraction of free, ample and excellent Aussie food and drink, and other freebies on hand (including a very cute toy Koala that travelled home with me the next day).

It may have been the delightful serendipity of the revelation that one of my companions from South Tees was (in addition to being the Deputy Mayor of Captain James Cook's hometown of Middlesbrough, which therefore gave us a tenuous excuse for us being at a reception we hadn't actually been invited to) also a native born Aussie herself!
A status derived from an abortive emigration to that fair continent by her family before a return to the delights (of which there are many) of Teesside. All of which arguably gave us far better reason to be at that reception than most of the other attendees there. Gatecrashers or not.

Whatever it was: drink, good fortune or the high spirits borne of outrageous coincidence, the speech given by Liz Truss, more a greeting and thank you to the Australian ambassador after their joint work on an Anglo-Aussie trade deal, was off-the-cuff, relaxed and surprisingly good.

It's a shame that this was arguably, from my perspective at least, the high point of Liz Truss' political career. For it was certainly mostly downhill after that.

The fact that the Conservative Party chose Liz Truss as its leader, and of course the debacle that followed, is illuminating of many of the traits, and all of the flaws, of the party in its current state. And a state it truly is in.

The major attraction of Truss to the party membership seems to have been a strange, and false, nostalgia for Margaret Thatcher, something that Truss bizarrely and memorably played up to in the first leadership debate by indulging in full-on cosplay in the role of the Iron Lady. Her blue, two piece suit dress, frilly shirt and pearls (were there pearls?) certainly tapped into the primal Thatcher look, earlier in her premiership before the late 80s power dressing and Aquascutum suits took centre stage. It was a striking image that must have been designed to dazzle the membership and distract from her laboured and uncertain debating style. It certainly worked.

The fact that umpteen Tory grandees, including Thatcher's former Chancellor Nigel Lawson, and many other people who had actually worked with Margaret Thatcher in her prime, lined up to point out that Truss was nothing like Thatcher in terms of personal style or character seemed to count for nothing with a membership longing for a return to Thatcherite certainty in the modern world.

As did the equally clear pronouncements of one-time ardent Thatcherites from the 1980s that Truss' announced policy platform was actually deeply un-Thatcherite, with its uncosted rush to tax cuts for the very richest, while inflation was still the dragon that any true heir to Thatcher would choose to slay first.

Superficially, Liz Truss looked Thatcherite, both in terms of policy and persona, and a Tory membership still reeling from the loss of their bumptious champion Boris Johnson might be forgiven for clinging to the comfort blanket of this Thatcher tribute act and the over-simplistic economics ('Trussonomics') that promised rapid growth born of instant tax cuts for the very richest in society.

They can be forgiven for the comforting choice they made perhaps, but not for the chaos that followed. Almost inevitably if the siren voices of Rishi Sunak and his supporters, and the orthodox Thatcherites were to be believed. A membership once lauded as one of the most sophisticated electorates in the world had clearly declined from its prime.

Others who should have known better, including some of our local MPs plumped for Truss for whatever reason: doctrinal or sentimental, or in the case of Simon Clarke MP possibly also personal, as this one time number two in the Treasury alongside Rishi Sunak as Chancellor seemed strangely detached from his one time boss. Simon's almost slavish devotion to Boris Johnson probably explains this enmity given Rishi's role in the clown's downfall, though there may be more at work.

Although Truss's victory secured Simon his place at the Cabinet table as Levelling Up Secretary, that success was to be short lived, as the Truss experiment imploded in remarkable short time and Simon then naturally, and foolishly, threw his lot in with the abortive Boris Beta 2 version that threatened to tear the Tory party apart, before sanity (or what passes for it in the current Tory party) prevailed.

Simon as a result languishes on the backbenches, part of the Johnsonite rump given to sniping and making life uncomfortable for Sunak in recent months. It's a sad result for a man I always found to be intelligent and hardworking, but entirely unsurprising given his utterly dreadful judgement in supporting both Johnson and Truss to the, very, bitter end. This was an habitual poor judgement that became clear from working with Simon Clarke as his Chairman and which he has recently reconfirmed.

For this incredibly poor judgement became even more evident in January 2024 when Simon Clarke launched what looks like a one-man, kamikaze, suicide mission against Rishi Sunak's leadership. In an article for the Daily Telegraph (which appears to have a clear agenda in trying to depose Sunak as Tory leader, for whatever motive) Simon declared that the Conservative Party was facing a 'massacre' followed by a 'decade of decline at the upcoming general election and that only a(nother) change of leadership could save the party.

Simon stated that Sunak's 'uninspiring leadership' was the main cause of the Tories dire polling (languishing around 20% support in most recent polls) and that Sunak needed to go as "he does not get what Britain needs. And he is not listening to what the British people want."

Simon stated elsewhere that he was acting alone and that, and the furiously negative response to his actions from almost all Tory MPs, make the 'kamikaze' label all the more apt. Even other right-wing critics of Sunak and potential rivals slammed Clarke's actions and opinion, Priti Patel stating that "engaging in facile and divisive self-indulgence only serves our opponents." David Davis, a fellow brexiteer of Clarke's was equally dismissive and government minister, and fellow North Yorkshire MP, Kevin Hollinrake described his intervention as 'panic', which was present in certain factions in the party but not widely shared.

As such Clarke's 'rebellion of one' appears to have gone down like a lead balloon with almost all MPs in his party, with only the usual suspects in the Boris Johnson Fanclub, Nadine Dorries and Andrea Jenkins speaking in support. So bad is Simon's judgement that he risks his entire future career being relegated to being part of such a backing act to Boris's faded pantomime clown.

For by 2024 a Johnson revival much desired by Clarke is now not just a ship that has sailed, but a ship that has sunk. The once ebullient Johnson now reduced to making dishevelled and seemingly half-cut mobile phone promos for his Daily Mail column from the back of an Uber, promoting such newspaper articles as to why he thinks another Trump presidency would be a good thing. Reason has clearly left the building when it comes to both Boris and his adoring admirers.

Clarke's intervention, claimed that yet another poisonous leadership contest and change of leader (creating a fourth PM since 2019 with only one of them actually endorsed by the voting public) would improve the Tory party's abysmal polling. This suggestion, of course, flies in the face of that cardinal rule beloved of political commentators and sephologists alike, that voters hate divided political parties and punish them accordingly at the ballot box. As such it stands as only the most recent example, but perhaps most glaring, of Clarke's appallingly bad judgement. Judgement that has probably ruined the career chances of a guy, who for all his faults, is undoubtedly able and intelligent.

I suspect Clarke's intervention, if it genuinely was a lone act, was a desperate last throw of the dice before he announces he will not be contesting his seat at the next election.

For the polling looks dreadful for Middlesbrough South and East Cleveland (MSEC), where ostensibly Clarke enjoys a 12,000 vote majority over Labour. The unfortunate reality for Clarke however, given what I gleaned from talking to umpteen voters there during the 2019 election, is that most of that was a pro-brexit, anti-Corbyn vote, rather than a positive vote for Clarke or the Conservative Party.

Given Brexit is done (for better or worse) Corbyn is history, and the Tories (Clarke himself of course bares considerable personal responsibility for this) have presided over a period of shambolic chaos in government, the omens, and predictions on Clarke's beloved 'Electoral Calculus' website don't look good for his chances of retaining his seat.

A well paid job in the law or City may be more appealing to Simon than fighting it out and facing likely defeat to Labour in MSEC, and maybe another part of his lone assault on Sunak was an attempt to raise his profile for prospective employers. If so, it's yet another example of Simon's extremely poor judgement that his one man rebellion has left him looking foolish and unsupported.

It's not a good look, but it does confirm all my worst impressions of Clarke's judgement, and so for that appallingly selfish reason I'm grateful for his recent kamikaze-like intervention. The problem with being 6 ft 7 tall is when you stick your head above the parapet you're more likely to get it blown off. As Simon has proved.

(As an aside, but on the same gigantism theme, I have a pet theory that may help to explain the cold relationship between Sunak and Clarke, quite apart from Clarke's perception of Sunak as the political assassin of his hero Boris Johnson. While it may appear ludicrous at first sight (no pun intended, read on) please indulge me:
Simon, as mentioned, is a gawky Six foot seven inches tall (the same as me, though I'm slightly fatter) Rishi is five foot nothing, and it's fair to say that together they look a very odd couple in official photographs. (One of the suspiciously few photos of them together, in front of an impressive Treasury fireplace when Clarke was the former Chancellor's deputy amusingly resurfaced in Clarke's MSEC newsletter, plopping onto my doormat on the very day Clarke launched his ill-fated assault.)

Famously, Simon was missing from the Treasury team in Sunak's budget photo outside Number 11, the team looking remarkably symmetrical and uniform in height in his absence. Simon's absence was later explained as being due to his agoraphobia, which was news to me; a condition that had never revealed itself in umpteen campaign stints in public together, but we must take such matters with seriousness and sincerity. But it may also be that Sunak is a little bit OCD and the thought of Simon spoiling his big-day photo by lurking asymmetrically on one side might just have been too much for Rishi to bear!)

But let us leave Clarke and Sunak's relationship at the heart of government fiscal and economic policy behind as we return to Truss and Kwarteng's rather more novel approach to economics. For in the 2022 leadership election and chaos that followed Truss' economic policy was viewed as reheated Reaganomics by many commentators and critics, myself included.

I also made the point on twitter, at the time and before the debacle of the Kwarteng mini-non-budget, that whilst Reaganomics might work when you have the world's reserve currency, the dollar, in support, it was likely to end badly when you only have the pound to fall back upon. And so it proved.

Simon Clarke later wrote an article in The Critic magazine making the same point and recounting how he had tried to convince Truss of the need for swinging public spending cuts to support the tax cuts for the highest earners that were a central part of the mini-non-budget. This is an interesting, even principled, standpoint for an MP for a constituency in one of the more deprived, and public-spending-reliant parts of the country, brave even. Especially in a cost of living crisis that has seen many working people fear for their ability to provide for their families.

For whilst Simon is himself wealthy and a high earner and therefore would have personally benefited from the Truss higher rate tax cut, paying for it by spending cuts to vital public services that his own electorate depended upon would surely have been a hard sell. There's that poor political judgement again, and I fully expect Simon's Labour opponent will make use of his line of argument on tax cuts for the rich and public spending cuts for everyone else, in the upcoming election in MSEC. Which is likely to be very close.

As for Truss and her administration it became clear that cosplay is no substitute for genuine intellectual depth, ability, realism and steely determination. Truss was known by some of those who had worked with her in the past as the 'human hand grenade' - such was her proclivity of liking to cause chaos as part of some odd creative process. As her premiership demonstrated, the chaos was real, but the creativity illusory.

By the time of the ouster of Boris Johnson and the leadership contest that followed, I had become so disenchanted by the state of the Conservative Party that I had resigned my membership. Even the two pounds and tuppence a month membership fee was too much to pay for the shambles that was unfolding before everybody's eyes. As such I had no vote in the leadership contest and will accept no responsibility for the, albeit mercifully brief, shitshow that unfolded under Truss. For the record, I would have voted for Rishi Sunak in that contest, limited though he is.

Truss' entire persona I found off putting; the vagueness and awkwardness noted above, but it's fair to say I had doctrinal differences too. Truss' embrace of the kind of hardline free-marketeer dogma she wrapped herself in wasn't attractive to a more mainstream Tory such as myself.

The market undoubtedly does offer answers to many problems facing the UK in the type of mixed economy most successful modern nations practice. What the market does well, it does well, but it's certainly not a cure-all, and has many flaws. So the kind of goggle-eyed, Taliban-style worshipping of the free market practised by Truss, Kwarteng and Clarke seems totally oblivious to the failings of the market (privatised water companies anyone?)

But even if I was a dyed-in-the-wool Thatcherite (I'm not, though I recognise that many of the radical reforms she introduced in the 1980s were necessary to break the post-war-consensus malaise that had set in) I wouldn't have supported Truss either. For her policy positions and approach simply weren't Thatcherite either. It was a messed up, juvenile, low-rent tribute act version of Thatcherism.

Indulging overly-simplistic adolescent fantasies on a free market economy, without accepting any of the realities of the market that underpin such thinking, is dangerous, as events would prove. It is also fantasy economics, based on trickle down theories almost entirely discredited anywhere outside of the kind of deluded think tanks such as Institute of Economic Affairs where Truss and Co cut their teeth.

As a foretaste of the mess to come, Truss and Kwarteng's contributions to 'Britannia Unchained' gave an indication of just how limited and blinkered their thinking was. They bear full responsibility for the damage to the UK, our economy and our people that followed their half-arsed and badly implemented plans. Enablers such as Simon Clarke share some of that responsibility too, for all his attempts to extricate himself from the blame with his erratum noted above.

Truss' notorious description of British workers as shirkers and workshy captured on audio recorded in 2019, and leaked during the leadership campaign, was sadly about as deep as her economic thinking got, and was reason enough for any truly patriotic Brit to reject her leadership bid.

Likewise, her plans for regional pay announced during the campaign and then swiftly rowed back on and denied, proved just how limited her thinking was and just how weak her taste for sticking to her guns in a fight was too. It should have been warning enough to Conservatives at all levels in the party, but sadly a nostalgic attraction to the cosplay seems to have blinded the party's ageing membership to the awkward truth about just who Truss really was.

As the 'semi-professional Yorkshireman' I am, the kind who loves to bang on about and sentimentally claim anything of worth from 'God's Own Country' the fact Truss grew up in Leeds causes me some discomfort. The fact she was born elsewhere in the country luckily offers a Yorkie get-out-clause because there's no way any self-respecting Yorkshireperson would want to take responsibility for Truss and the mess she created.

What is more, her false characterisation of her own school in the well-to-do Leeds suburb of Roundhay as a failing school that let its pupils down should also have been warning enough of Truss' relaxed relationship with the truth. Though standards on this are clearly relative in the modern Conservative Party after its embrace of Johnsonism.

So, all in all, it's fair to say the warning signs were there long before Truss walked through the doors of Downing Street to put into action her agenda, for which it should of course be noted she had absolutely no popular mandate. The fact her plans seemed ill-thought through to so many observers from across the political spectrum was a bad omen, though I don't think anyone prior to her 49 days in power had suggested they would also be quite so catastrophically implemented.

Kwarteng's mini-non-budget, so phrased in order to evade the usual scrutiny of the Office for Budget Responsibility, was economically terrible in terms of market-spooking fiscal content, and politically inept in terms of prioritising tax cuts for the very richest at a time of genuine financial strain for most mere-mortal Brits.

The fact it not only evaded OBR scrutiny, but that Kwarteng failed to follow the tradition of running its main points past the Governor of the Bank of England before the big reveal was evidence not just of a disdain for 'experts' but a truly reckless disregard for norms of behaviour. Sensible norms established through years of practice to lessen the danger of the chaos that actually then ensued once those norms had been ignored. Utterly reckless.

The fact Kwarteng later doubled down on the market disquiet by promising more to come was beyond reckless, and the results predictable.

This would be bad enough if it was just reputational damage to the Tory party that resulted but of course there were real world effects too, harms caused to real people just unlucky enough to be caught up in the student politics and inept economics of Truss and co.

When Truss bowed to market reaction and internal party pressure, and called Kwarteng back from Washington to be sacked in a ritual sacrifice to appease their detractors she as good as signed her own resignation letter at the same time, as Kwarteng apparently predicted to her. One thing, at least, that he did get right. The fact she felt it necessary to replace him with an old hand from the other wing of the party in Jeremy Hunt simply made her position look all the weaker.

For it was here that the two pillars of the fake Thatcher cosplay collided: Truss' policies simply weren't Thatcherite and she lacked Thatcher's steely resolve to see her policies through once they proved unpopular and had negative market consequences. Thatcher famously faced down her own critics both within the party and in the markets and schools of economics when the initial effects of her monetarist policies appeared disastrously counter-productive in the early 1980s. She had the resolve to face them down and soldier on. Truss on the other hand scarpered at the first whiff of gunsmoke.

As if this wasn't bad enough, so much so to bring down a premiership, it's often forgotten that Truss was't brought down by the economic mess she had wrought alone. There was further leadership incompetence to come as her government tripped up over an obvious elephant trap set for it by the Labour party.

The issue was fracking, a source of energy which has transformed US reliance on overseas fuel but with allegedly calamitous environmental side effects in the vast open spaces of North America. As such it's an idea much beloved by some on the hard right of the Tory party who don't seem to realise that the UK is a tiny, crowded, already much environmentally denuded place compared to the US.

Or maybe they can just whiff the money likely to come their way and are confident enough that no fracking plants will find themselves placed anywhere near their country estates. In fairness to Kwarteng (you know me, always fair) as a former Energy Secretary he was aware of the very limited positive impact fracking could have on UK energy supplies without massive (and massively unpopular) environmental damage alongside it. Other members of the Truss cabal such as Jacob Rees-Mogg were ardent supporters however, and it was these divisions a Labour Commons motion rather cleverly sought to exacerbate.

This was nonetheless a clear elephant trap that any half-competent government should be able to negotiate successfully, but which unfortunately the Truss government blundered straight into through its trademark mixed messaging and confusion. By way of cosplay comparison, if Margaret Thatcher was famously, in Dennis Healey's words, the 'Great She-Elephant' of the Tory Party she was at least deft enough never to fall for such a blatant trap as that which Truss plunged into.

Was it a vote of confidence in Truss' already embattled government or not? At first it was, and then it wasn't. Or maybe that should be at first it wasn't and then it was? Either way, it then changed and was or wasn't again, if you catch my drift, and frankly I'm confused just recounting it.

Junior ministers said one thing in the debate and the Whips office said another. Chief Whip Wendy Morton, who I know personally from campaigning for her in Tynemouth in the 2010 election, is a very personable and able individual but would never have struck me as a first choice for Chief Whip. Another of Truss' numerous mistakes as cosplay PM was in only selecting members of Cabinet from among her own supporters in the leadership election. This not only offended the majority of Tory MPs who never backed her but also restricted the pool of talent from which to choose. Too many Trussite square pegs seem to have ended up in too many round holes in government as a result.

Accounts persist of Tory MPs being harangued and denounced by Truss supporting ministers, and in some cases physically manhandled into the voting lobbies in scenes more befitting a Balkan assembly than the Mother of Parliaments. Jacob Rees-Mogg and Therese Coffey being mentioned among the alleged 'heavies' in some of the chaotic scenes. A pairing quite alarming of itself, in an Addams Family kind of way.

Whatever the numerical result of the non binding vote on Labour's fracking motion, the practical result was the resignation of Wendy

Morton as Chief Whip and the Deputy Chief Whip in response to the chaotic lack of leadership from Truss and Number Ten. The evening's entertainment in the 'Palace of Varieties' apparently concluded with Truss running down a Westminster corridor after her former Chief Whip screeching "Wendy, please don't go!"

All very dramatic in an Eastenders, 'dum, dum, dum, dum' finale kind of way, but it was clear from that moment that the Truss premiership was well and truly fracked.

By the following day Truss was visited by Sir Graham Brady of the 1922 Committee of backbench Tory MPs to tell her the writing was on the wall and the traditional 'pearl handled revolver' was being dusted off, and she should do the decent thing and resign.

Which to her credit she did. Perhaps the only thing of credit she did. But her swift passing was entirely fighting her brief stint as PM, all of 49 days, the shortest in British history, and a pub quiz question down your local for evermore. A fitting memorial.

So what does the Truss premiership tell us about the current Conservative Party beyond its members' nostalgic liking for Thatcher cosplay?

For one thing, there is a clear and potentially dangerous disconnect between the thinking of the membership and MPs on both policy and competency when it comes to leadership elections. Members want full-blooded Thatcherism, even if it's actually only the 'Thatcheresque' they get rather than the real thing.

Rather as Corbyn's election as Labour leader showed Labour members and activists to be well to the left of their MPs, Truss' election shows Tory members to be well to the right of the Conservative parliamentary party. This is not unusual in British political parties, and it's also common for those who take the trouble to become members and activists to have much stronger views than those who merely vote for a given party at elections.

But the real danger here, especially having been denied a say in Rishi Sunaks's coronation in replacement of Truss, is that after the likely election defeat this year, the Tory party membership will follow the Corbynistas in electing a leader on the political extreme of their party who will appeal to their doctrinaire beliefs, but who will prove repellent to voters. A longer period in opposition than strictly necessary will be the result. Doctrinaire leaders tend to take their parties on a long march to ideological purity that pleases the members but is disastrous electorally, and from whence it's a long trek back to actual power.

Any attempt to thwart this by the party establishment could well result in the party splitting entirely. So many members I have known have come into the current party from Ukip, and many would actually be far more comfortable in Reform if they cannot mould the Tory party to their outlook. Several MPs are of the same ilk, not least Simon Clarke himself. On the flip side many traditional Tories have either left or been thrown out over Brexit, and find themselves homeless on the centre-right. Such a split may well please them and those who remain on the One Nation wing of the party, but under our electoral system any such split on the right is likely to be as damaging to electoral chances as the Labour-Lib Dem division on the left has been.

The Truss debacle was a symptom of a much wider malaise in what was once regarded as the natural party of government in Britain. The long standing 'broad church' accommodation between left and right in the party appears to have broken down, largely over Brexit but also encompassing the older split between Thatcherites (or their wannabees) and the Tory mainstream. The Truss premiership was both a symptom of that and a likely cause of further divergence. Truss' approach has discredited Thatcherite ideas for the time being, but the true believers are still there, and more numerous among the membership, and their desire to rehabilitate those ideas from the Truss debacle will likely cause friction with the more One Nation wing of the party.

In short, the Truss experience was a party that has largely lost its way dealing with the realities of a low growth and high demand ageing nation and seeking to cling to certainties of old that, in truth, are past their best. Especially when carried out in a half-arsed fashion. The membership still cling to that ideal though, and given the likely demise of the Sunak government and his more mainstream approach in the coming election, a Truss Mark Two is the most likely outcome for the party.

In place of Truss' chaos, ineptitude and lack of resolve it will likely have a much harder, not to say, unpleasant edge, especially if Suella Braverman follows through on her challenges to Sunak and the resultant engineered sacking with a successful run for the leadership.

In place of Truss veneer-thin certainty, Braverman has an almost unbearable arrogance and belief in her own blinkered view of the world that may please members but is likely to prove extremely off-putting to voters. This aspect of her character, and the view among many even on the Tory Right that she has overplayed her hand in her tussle with Sunak may well see another champion of that wing of the party emerge victorious, and Kemi Badenoch appears a favourite with many members. It would certainly be a striking choice of leader for the Conservative Party but perhaps a natural progression for a 'conservative' party which has never been frightened to break with convention in recognising genuine talent. However, lack of experience and lack of exposure if combined with overly doctrinaire right wing views is not a great recipe for success.

The party and its new leadership which will emerge is likely to prove more disciplined and less chaotic than the Truss experiment but barring a major social and economic catastrophe under Labour and Starmer, it is unlikely to see the Tories return to power any time soon.

Update

In early February 2024, Liz Truss headed up the launch of yet another Conservative faction, this one being 'Popular Conservatism'. I sense that Liz Truss doesn't 'do' irony but her heading up the 'Popular Conservatives' is dripping with irony of the most delicious kind.

Sadly, Sir Simon Clarke had been uninvited from the launch following his one man suicide mission against Rishi Sunak's leadership the previous month. Simon now seems to be in a faction of one.

Chapter 10 - Without a Leg to Stand On

Pinchinthorpe Hall is a stately country house situated in the countryside between industrial Teesside and the dramatic 'dragon's back' of the Cleveland Hills, that rise and fall majestically to the south. A modest but historic manor it pales in comparison to the much grander Gisborough Hall in the nearby market town of Guisborough (note the differing spellings, and overlook at your peril) seat of Lord Gisborough, a kindly old aristo and also a member of South Tees Conservative Association.

In early 2022 Pinchinthorpe Hall had been selected as the venue for the association's annual dinner, the organisers (largely me, as our Social Secretary, Cllr Andrea Turner seemed to have fallen out with me and gone awol) were attracted by its private country house feel. Less commercial than its near neighbour, it well suited our aim of providing a high-end but intimate setting for the festivities. Its ambience would also have worked well for a murder-mystery evening, though given the ever fractious nature of the local Conservative party, the fictionalised role play might easily have taken a more truly homicidal turn.

The hall was genuinely historic in its own right, as the owner and events manager, Simon, pointed out on a planning visit. One old sandstone doorway, in that gorgeous honey-coloured stone so common to the area, bore the sword marks of Civil War cavaliers who apparently sharpened their sabres on the way out to join the nearby Battle of Guisborough on 16th January 1643.

The fact that the battle was won overwhelmingly by Parliamentarian forces over the old Tory Royalists may have been a bad omen for a Conservative Party annual dinner (members have long memories!) but the venue was so fitting for what we were looking for that any concerns were swept aside.

The further fact that the Royalist commander on the day had both his legs blown off by cannon-fire during the battle could also have been regarded as a bad omen. Though I'm sure he wasn't the last person to end up legless at a Conservative Party social venue. Boom, boom!

As it turned out the omen proved highly prophetic of events to come later that year, as our esteemed guest speaker for the function was one Right Honourable Kwasi Kwarteng MP, fittingly a published historian himself.

At the time he was Business Secretary, his later elevation to Chancellor of the Exchequer by the equally ill-fated Liz Truss, and their calamitous non-budget, would lead to a run in with the markets, the 'experts' and economic reality, which would also leave them both without a leg to stand on.

As it was, the local association was grateful for his presence at all, the guests for our last two functions having cried off at late notice (Tees Valley Mayor Ben Houchen, understandably, following two deaths in an explosion at the Teesworks site) or simply forgotten to turn up at all (you know who you are, Lord Callanan!)

By all accounts Kwasi was a charming and attentive guest, going table to table after the meal to speak to attendees and having delivered a well regarded after-dinner speech. I say by all accounts as I did not attend the event that I, ironically, had done so much to organise. My falling out with the party nationally had occurred a few weeks earlier, and I had cancelled my £2.02 per month membership Direct Debit and certainly wasn't going to contribute another £90 to party coffers, even with a glass of prosecco thrown in.

I understand the mention of my name at the dinner was greeted with a hearty cheer from members and local party colleagues, which is genuinely touching and a mark of the real friendships I had with many of those present. I suspect, however, such a mention would elicit a groan or even boos now, given my more recent activities (though I am still on good terms with a number of local members)

As mentioned, Kwasi Kwarteng is a published historian with a specialism in economic history, which makes the debacle that followed in the autumn of that year all the more perplexing and embarrassing.

Kwasi is also an example of how the Conservative Party's laudable drive for diversity is of a somewhat limited nature. A black man, child of Ghanaian immigrants, he is one of an encouraging number of ethnic minority MPs in a party that was undoubtedly once upon a time (and to a much lesser extent now) riddled with racial prejudice. However, the fact that he is also an Old Etonian (albeit on a scholarship) speaks of the superficial nature of that diversity: the Tory party is still highly class-bound with a noticeable proportion of its MPs coming from an upper-middle class and public school background.

This is markedly so among the ethnic minority MPs within the current party; they are very much of a particular class and educational background (Rishi Sunak is a case in point, his excruciating teenage interview about his lack of working class friends serving as stark illustration.)

Put simply, I fear Kwasi would have struggled to rise within the Conservative Party had he grown up in a working-class family in Brixton and attended a bog-standard (to use New-Labour terminology) comprehensive school. This is the social and political reality of Britain today which is still very far from being the meritocracy that it should be. The damaging consequences of this can be seen on the societal level in terms of the dreadful performance of UK plc under its public-school/Oxbridge leadership (comprehensive school and Oxbridge girl Liz Truss is perhaps the exception that proves the rule)

On an individual level it also serves to frustrate those of talent from more modest backgrounds who are undoubtedly still passed over in favour of those who went to the right schools and/or had the wealth and connections to get on in a society that is still appallingly class-ridden. If you don't believe the whinging of this clearly very embittered former comprehensive school and new-university boy, then you need merely check out the educational and social data for all the leading careers, be it the law, senior civil service, journalism, banking, business, and bizarrely now even acting (hello Benedict and Eddie)

In addition to his historical works, Kwasi was also one of five contributing writers to 2012's 'Britannia Unchained', the Conservative right-wing political and economic treatise now more widely regarded, after Liz and Kwasi's attempted implementation of its ideas, as 'Britannia Unhinged.'

The quintet of authors also included fellow one-time Cabinet members Dominic Raab and Priti Patel, and the less successful (if that is possible) Chris Skidmore. Each were of the 2010 intake of Conservative MPs and it might have been better they'd waited a few more years before setting out their rather flaky rehash of Thatcherite free-market economics in the book. Even better if they hadn't caused serious damage to the British economy and the Conservative Party's reputation (not to mention actual people's real lives) by their half-arsed attempted implementation of the book's ideas in autumn 2022.

The tome included the passage:

"The British are among the worst idlers in the world. We work among the lowest hours, we retire early and our productivity is poor. Whereas Indian children aspire to be doctors or businessmen, the British are more interested in football and pop music."

which pretty much sums up the intellectual 'depth' of the book and rather amusingly came back to bite Liz Truss on the backside during her leadership bid in summer of that year. Less amusing was the fact that her bid was successful and such views clearly found support among an out-of-touch Conservative Party membership (largely retired)

The UK undoubtedly does face serious economic, social and political problems and underperforms across a whole range of international measures. However, the belief that solutions to those problems can simply be cut and pasted from what works in vastly different societies such as Hong Kong or Singapore (much less from the pages of a reheated-Thatcherite treatise by student politicians such as Truss) is both simplistic and offensive. Not least to the very people actually working hard, often for chronically low wages, to keep UK plc afloat. The so-called 'idlers' of 'Britannia Unhinged'.

Anyway, least said, soonest mended, although it's likely that a Conservative defeat at the next election (an almost odds on certainly) will bring such threadbare ideas back to the fore. This is especially so if, given the party membership, the party swings to the right, possibly even to one of the aforementioned authors, Priti Patel, whose star, is at time of writing, on the rise again given Suella Braverman's recent meltdown.

The tendency of Liz Truss, unlike Kwasi, to continue to give speeches defending her time in office also suggests an unapologetic air to those on the free-market right of the party that does not bode well for the party's future. Nothing seems to have been learned by Truss and her supporters other than the false lesson that the problem was only in the poor communication of their policies rather than the policies and their implementation itself. Or, even worse, blamed on liberal 'deep state' opposition.

True, the communication *was* dreadful from both Truss and Kwarteng, Truss in her inherent wet-rag lack of communication skills and Kwarteng in his further spooking of already panicked markets with his reckless promise of 'more to come'. But fundamentally, the policy programme itself was wrongheaded from the start, and doomed to failure as even any third rate economics student such as myself could see.

As discussed earlier, it wasn't *even* true reheated-Thatcherism that Truss and Kwarteng attempted in autumn 2022. As many of Thatcher's actual colleagues pointed out at the time, the policies were deeply un-Thatcherite in themselves, involving as they did unfunded tax cuts (for the very wealthiest only, note) at a time when inflation was the greatest risk to economic recovery. Thatcher, love her or loathe her (or somewhere in between if you're like me) delayed tax cuts in the 1980s until inflation was tackled and was above all else about sound government finances and living within your means

No, the Truss/Kwarteng 'non-budget' programme of 2022 was a doomed-to-failure reheated 'Reaganomics' approach that undoubtedly pleased wealthy members of the Conservative Party, but crucially lacked the little matter of the world's reserve currency, the US dollar, which made Reaganomics viable. This is no hindsight at work, but was pointed out in advance by various people, not least yours truly.

As an Eton-educated, published historian with a specialism in economic history one might have hoped Kwasi Kwarteng would also have spotted all of this well in advance. The fact he didn't rather confirms my central thesis (prejudice?) that it's the over-promotion of public school educated types, with the right connections, in UK society that is holding UK Plc back, far more than its poor benighted workers. Until this changes, and opportunities are made available truly based on merit rather than social class and background, Britain's progress is likely to remain stunted.

Update

In early February 2024, and annoyingly for Liz Truss who was due to launch her 'Popular Conservative' gang the day after, Kwazi Kwarteng announced to his own local association that he would not be contesting his Surrey seat at the next general election. Given his chaotic stint as Chancellor and the veritable exodus of other sitting Conservative MPs also announcing they were stepping down at the election this was perhaps unsurprising.

Chapter 11 - Imran Khan

No. Not THAT Imran Khan.

I have no personal knowledge whatsoever of former Pakistan Prime Minister and international cricketer, Imran Khan. I do know he was a far better cricketer than politician, and a talented foe for a usually hapless England cricket team in the 1980s and 90s. Given the similar calamitous state of Pakistan politics his achievement in rising to power, with army help, should perhaps not be underestimated. Though his recent fall from power, and later imprisonment, also with army help, shouldn't be overlooked either.

I do sympathise with being confused with others who share the same name however. I'm often confused with a certain Cllr Lee Holmes of Skelton in Cleveland, who has what might charitably be termed a 'colourful' social media history. I really *am not* him by the way.

But I digress.

No, the Imran Khan I have knowledge of is one Imran Ahmad Khan, sometime Conservative MP for Wakefield, West Yorkshire.

In April 2022 this Imran Khan was convicted at Southwark Crown Court of the indecent assault of a 15 year old boy in 2008, at a boozy house party in Staffordshire.

In May 2022 Khan was sentenced to 18 months imprisonment for his crime, with the judge commenting upon his obvious lack of remorse.

The allegations accepted by the court stated that Khan had plied his young victim with gin before taking him upstairs at the party to watch pornography, before groping him on a bunk bed. The victim had reported it to police at the time but had decided not to press charges, and only subsequently came forward again to police following Khan's election as Wakefield's Conservative MP in December 2019.

When Khan was charged in 2021 another acquaintance of his came forward with allegations Khan had on one occasion shared a bedroom with him in Pakistan, that he had smoked marijuana with him, encouraged him to take sleeping tablets with a view to subduing him and that he had awoken to find Khan molesting him without his consent. These allegations were not put to the jury as part of the charges but the alleged victim's testimony was given as witness evidence and no doubt acted as significant corroboration of Khan's predilections.

The original victim had approached Conservative CCHQ during the 2019 general election after becoming aware that Khan had been selected to stand as the Conservative candidate in Wakefield. The victim said that when his phone call had been referred to a more senior figure in the Conservative Press Office the response had been dismissive of his allegations.

For the record, the party denies any knowledge of the victim's telephone contact. Ho hum.

At that late stage in the election process it may have been difficult, if not impossible, to get Khan's name off the ballot as the Conservative Party candidate and it may have been tempting to let sleeping dogs lie. Especially in a tight campaign in the new battleground of Red Wall seats in the north of England such as Wakefield. Only CCHQ staffers know the truth, and they ain't talking. However, this accusation of inaction confirms my own experience of a Conservative Party 'machine' that corruptly puts covering the party's back above safeguarding vulnerable young people from abuse.

Subsequent to Khan's conviction a further alleged victim has come forward to the Guardian newspaper alleging that Khan had propositioned him when he was only 16 years old, making offers of a variety of sexual services.

Much was made in Khan's defence and subsequent comments after conviction of the shame involved in being both muslim and gay, and having his alcohol consumption made public in proceedings. No doubt that is true, it is still difficult for many gay men in the UK to 'come out' and that difficulty is more difficult in more conservative faith communities such as Islam. However, it's no mitigation for the crime Khan was convicted of. Khan immediately announced he would appeal against his conviction, though he later announced he would step down as MP for Wakefield, prompting a potentially damaging by-election in this Red Wall Tory gain from 2019. (Subsequently lost to Labour in June 2022)

Tory MP Crispin Blunt, a now vocal campaigner for gay rights, and poppers use, initially declared the conviction a 'miscarriage of justice' and 'international scandal' to considerable controversy before rowing back, presumably after a chat with party managers. One time vociferously homophobic critics in the party such as Blunt, can often be the worst advocates for the gay community once they come out and accept their own sexuality. There's nothing worse than 'converts', as the old saying goes.

But all of the above begs the question of how the hell Khan ever became a parliamentary candidate, and later MP, for the party, and it's here that my own encounter with Khan comes in.

I met Khan at the 2019 Conservative Party Conference in Manchester, or more precisely on the city's famous Canal Street, heart of the gay village. Even more precisely, in G.A.Y nightclub, where the Tory LGBT society was hosting a (very enjoyable and subsidised-bar) social event. To a backdrop of cheesy disco tunes and high-heeled and feisty drag queens, the party faithful of a certain persuasion (and hangers-on in search of a good night out) partied into the early hours in that boozy way only Tories at conference can manage.

I had no idea who Khan was at the time (and until several months later following his election for Wakefield) when this curious figure in a grey three-piece suit and tottering on a walking cane appeared. He was pissed as a fart, clearly completely bonkers and with an equally drunk young companion, hanging on his every (very slurred) word and fawning over his 'brilliance'.

"He's the next Boris Johnson. He's the next Boris!" his young hanger-on would declare to anyone who would listen, and Khan was not one for contradiction, clearly basking in the adulation.

With hindsight this declaration of adoration for the man, and comparison with the 'Great Leader' himself, Boris Johnson, is even more stunningly, absurdly, hilarious than at first hearing. A prime example of delusions of grandeur, overblown sense of entitlement and fatal character flaws that, rather ironically, afflict both men. Whilst there is no suggestion of criminal sexual impropriety among the long charge sheet Boris faces from his critics, Boris undoubtedly has a colourful sexual history, with a string of failed marriages, affairs and barely acknowledged children in his past.

Given the largely achievement-free and untruth-strewn rise to power enjoyed by our erstwhile Prime Minister, and tendency towards the bizarre in modern politics, perhaps Ahmad Khan's adoring companion's ambitions were not as absurd as they seemed. A conviction for child sex offences notwithstanding, of course.

Khan *was* eloquent in a drunken and over-the-top kind of way. There was a likeness to Boris Johnson in his rotund, plummy-voiced, verbosity. Just like Boris, a kind of pantomime version of Falstaff.

He was, like Boris, entertaining as only British eccentrics can be, holding forth on various subjects and not missing a chance to expound on his own undisputed (in his own mind) talents. I passed a few minutes in his presence with several other amused onlookers before making my excuses and slipping away. Pantomime can be fun, but you wouldn't actually want your country to be run like one..

For, amusing as Khan undoubtedly was in his drunken state, he *was also* clearly utterly barmy. A strange cabaret act of extraordinary eccentricity and self-regard, with the plummy voice of the British upper class mixed with the unsteady gestures of a vaudeville drunk. And as such, quite wearing after a surprisingly short period of time.

So, how does such an obviously unsuitable individual, given his sober behaviour was apparently not much less eccentric than his drunken state, get through selection as a parliamentary candidate for the Conservative Party? Are some of the factors at work in the selection of David Smith for local elections in Middlesbrough repeated to some extent in the party nationally? What does this mean for our democracy?

Khan *did* have an interesting CV, apparently somewhat inflated in its claimed achievements and vague in other areas. Perhaps, some slack was cut on this given that his career seemed centred on 'security' work. There were some rumours that he may previously have been engaged in espionage work for the Foreign Office in the often volatile and dangerous borderlands of Pakistan and Afghanistan in the era of Taliban insurgency.

Colleagues in the field certainly spoke highly of his somewhat fearless approach to 'intelligence' work at ground level, gleaning the attitudes of his fellow muslims in Pakistan and Afghanistan. Though they also very much asserted that such intelligence was low-level and generic stuff.

Other career positions stated by Khan seem somewhat questionable given the seniority of the claimed employments and his own young age at the time. His educational career was marked by incomplete and dubiously claimed courses, according to reports following conviction in the Guardian newspaper.

But fundamentally, given all this, how did such an eccentric get through the Conservative Party's' expensive, involved and allegedly thorough recruitment process?

(There's no suggestion that at this stage the party was aware of any offending behaviour on the part of Khan, or of the crime for which he was subsequently convicted.)

Are the long and detailed application forms, mini biographies, group exercises and psychometric testing employed by the party actually effective in choosing able, talented and morally sound future MPs and weeding out those constitutionally unsuitable for the role? Certainly the succession of MP scandals which have dogged the party in recent years suggest its selection processes leave much to be desired.

But more than that, do the selection processes produce production-line, identikit candidates, with no *public* foibles, but little in the way of originality or challenging thought? Certainly, the particular circumstances of Khan's selection for Wakefield suggest that such a risk-averse, safety-first approach to candidates, rather ironically in this case, actually created a perfect example of 'out of the frying pan, into the fire'.

For Khan only became the Conservative candidate for Wakefield after the original candidate for that constituency was stood down by the party. This was done in an effort to avoid controversy, after some ill-judged, though arguably not hanging-offence, comments by that candidate on our old friend 'social media'. The party is now so in awe of the power of social media that any even slightly off-message tweet or facebook post seems magnified in its significance.

The original Conservative candidate for Wakefield, Antony Calvert, had, some years earlier (social media is eternal remember) posted some rather ungallant comments on Facebook about his Labour opponent, Mary Creagh, the incumbent MP.

Commenting on her appearance on a BBC politics programme back in 2010 he had stated "Can't believe just how shocking Mary Creagh looks on TV. Obviously the BBC makeup department doesn't work on a Sunday." So far, so bitchy. Possibly also evidence of a disturbing misogyny in this day and age. Or possibly just a failed attempt at humour (a dangerous thing in modern politics, as our own local MP Jacob Young found out when he humorously commented on his first post-lockdown haircut with a joke about 'Tory cuts' prompting howls of self-righteous indignation from the local Labour twitterati)

Calvert followed up on this dodgy sexist humour with a dangerously racist joke, in 2011, about how if Colonel Gaddaffi had wanted to go unrecognised on the street after his fall from power in Libya, he should have moved to Bradford. Not big and not clever, especially in the modern era of an 'offence culture' ready to go into overdrive at the slightest hint of an 'ism'.

So the party powers-that-be immediately reviewed Calverts candidacy when the offending tweets were exposed in early November 2019, about a month before polling day, and he was rapidly dropped in favour of Imran Ahmad Khan. In hindsight, the dodgy humour merchant was probably a less damaging choice than the highly eccentric 'character' with a penchant for young boys that they ended up with. But that's hindsight for you.

Certainly, I was astonished when several months after the 2019 General Election I saw Khan introduced as the new Conservative MP for Wakefield on a BBC news programme. His muslim name also came as a surprise given how drunk he was at the LGBT event at Tory conference some months earlier, though obviously some muslims are less observant than others.

How *had* this clearly unsuitable individual made it through the Conservative Party's parliamentary selection procedures? Had a plummy voice and public school education helped? Undoubtedly, because the Tory party is clearly still as class-bound as England in the 1950s, and such things still count for far more than they should in the 'modern' party (they should of course count for zilch in a well-run, centre-right party that believes in genuine meritocracy, but there you go.)

Quite how Imran Ahmad Khan, an eccentric fantasist with a liking for walking canes, three piece suits and referring to his mother as 'mammaaaar' was ever deemed suitable for the party's Candidates List is a question for the party's Candidate's Team and Candidates Committee. But good luck on ever getting an answer out of this byzantine organisation that views covering its back and admitting no wrong as its paramount concern. I failed to ever get any answers to my queries about how various paedophiles, sex pests and crooks got through a supposedly thorough and sophisticated selection process. You might fare better…

The serious point here, quite apart from keeping sexual predators and other criminals out of positions of trust, is that the reality of our electoral system means that only party candidates (George Galloway notwithstanding) have a real chance of being elected to parliament. As such, the party's have a virtual monopoly over which of our citizens stand a chance of being elected and in turn what kind of people we end up with, shaping the laws that control our lives and the policies that decide our livelihoods.

As such, we all have a vested interest in making sure the parties' processes are as fair and thorough as possible, and give rise to a wide variety of candidates who are truly representative of society in terms of background, education, career, race, gender, sexuality, faith and disability. If not, the quality of our democracy can only suffer.

Although I can only speak from my experience of the way the Conservative Party selects its candidates, and I really hope other parties do a better job, in my opinion the Conservative candidate selection processes and the team behind it are simply not fit for purpose, and the 'quality' of our elected representatives is proof of that

Chapter 12 - CCHQ and The Party

It would be unfair to suggest that the Conservative Party's Campaign HeadQuarters in London (CCHQ) was staffed entirely by the idiot children of wealthy donors to the Conservative Party, but this was certainly the impression it gave me in my numerous dealings with the party's HeadQuarters.

Simple requests, though often about very serious matters, usually went ignored and unanswered, and often with calamitous results. Muddled and mixed messaging were the order of the day when responses actually did arrive.

Once housed in the stately 1960s tower block at Millbank (also once home to the Labour Party in the Blair years) CCHQ had by then decamped to less imposing premises on Matthew Parker Street. As mentioned earlier, the building which acted as Tory HQ, seemed to act like a massive information black-hole, forever sucking in the info, often demanded and sent to it, from the numerous associations around the country, but rarely, if ever, letting anything of use escape its overwhelming gravitational pull.

Whether such 'info-retentiveness' was born of incompetence or active paranoia, I was never entirely able to discern. Probably a bit of both given the nature of the party in the 21st century. Certainly there seemed to be a paranoia about entrusting useful information to the oiks out in the regions who actually kept the party running. And incompetence there was aplenty.

Phone calls, when answered at all, which wasn't often, usually confused more than they clarified, as the often well-spoken teenagers, seemingly in their first hours of the job (or unpaid internship) struggled to comprehend what you wanted. Or quite possibly to comprehend anybody speaking with a regional accent.

The issue of unpaid internships has rightly become one of concern for those who believe in meritocracy and social mobility in the UK, as only those candidates from wealthier backgrounds can even afford to undertake them.

With the Conservative Party this issue is even more pressing given that only those already with connections in the party are likely to be accepted anyway, and in turn are more likely to emerge from CCHQ internships into special adviser or researcher positions and go on to become favoured candidates, and eventually MPs. This kind of 'golden circle' approach is bad for such social mobility, and given the dreadful state of the party and the country, clearly also bad for them too.

A good example of party ineptitude about really quite pressing matters was when I approached the CCHQ Candidates Team at the party conference in Manchester in early October 2019. As Deputy Chairman Political of South Tees Conservatives my remit was all things electoral, and with rumours of an imminent snap 'Brexit' election swirling, and no candidates chosen for either our Redcar or Middlesbrough constituencies it was potentially a crucial issue.

Middlesbrough is dyed-in-the-wool Labour territory, unlikely ever to flip blue, but in any election fought largely on 'getting Brexit done', to coin Johnson's much repeated slogan, the heavily Leave voting Redcar was an outside chance for the party. One where having a strong local candidate could potentially make all the difference. By October 2019 we had no candidate at all, nor any steer from CCHQ on appointing one.

Having approached a senior member of the Candidate's Team at their conference hall stand I was passed on to a junior staffer in charge of the laptop and spreadsheet upon which the party's candidate plans for every constituency in the UK were stored. Having explained my interest in Redcar constituency in my capacity as DCP of South Tees, the young lady struggled, and failed, to find any listing whatsoever for Redcar.

It simply wasn't there among the Conservative Party's 'detailed' plans for winning a Brexit general election. A tad insulting to the good folk of Redcar, who as it happened were soon to return the first Conservative MP in their history.

Or if it was there on the party's database, this hapless young staffer couldn't find any mention of it, which is little better.

One could, with a northerner's chip on one's shoulder (I have two, one on each, being a well balanced individual) regard this as typical of a Tory Party long dominated by the south east of England and with little traditional interest in 'the North'. Or it could be just yet another indication of just how shambolic CCHQ, and the Candidate's Team, generally are.

Needless to say, when the mooted general election was called just a month later, we had no candidate for Redcar, let alone Middlesbrough, nor were we allowed to choose any candidates for either, as the party imposed its own choices upon the association.

This may have been a deliberate ploy, favoured by CCHQ in snap elections, to keep the choice out of the hands of local associations, who clearly aren't regarded as being trustworthy enough to choose wisely. Or it could have been ineptitude. My money is on the latter, with an undercurrent of the former.

One candidate so imposed, was Jacob Young, who would subsequently go on to become Redcar's first Tory MP.

I understand that Jacob had initially applied to become the Tory candidate in more winnable seats in the north of England, Penrith constituency in Cumbria was mentioned, having stood at two general elections already despite only still being in his early twenties. When he proved unsuccessful in this he reluctantly agreed to be the party's candidate in Redcar once again, having stood there in 2015. He had apparently refused point blank to run again in Middlesbrough, having been the candidate there in his hometown in the 2017 election. We've had so many elections in recent years that keeping track has become a challenge in itself.

Middlesbrough constituency had a candidate with no links to the town or region whatsoever parachuted in at the last minute, in the traditional CCHQ practice of throwing a brand new candidate into an unwinnable seat purely to gain experience for later contests.

Ruth Betson, the candidate imposed, was from Cambridgeshire and unfortunately came unstuck in one of the few Middlesbrough campaigning events she was allowed by CCHQ, when eagle eyed locals spotted that the 'local voter' she was photographed meeting was actually a delightful and long-standing Conservative Party activist who unfortunately didn't actually live in Middlesbrough constituency either.

Ruth was a very pleasant individual, who's ardent Brexiteer views would have chimed well with many in Middlesbrough. Sadly though, on the one canvassing session she undertook, alongside yours truly and a local press reporter, in an otherwise positive outing in a frigid Acklam, Middlesbrough, the disappointment from voters when she answered the inevitable question about if she was from the area in the negative, was audible.

Some local councillors felt that a strong local candidate might have had an outside chance of winning even Middlesbrough from Labour, and although I'm sceptical about this, we'll never know.

This rather amateurish approach by CCHQ to candidate selection and targeting winnable seats luckily didn't cost the party the 2019 election, so overwhelming were the issues at stake, but unless CCHQ has dramatically improved in these things since, it doesn't augur well for a much tighter, or in all likelihood do-or-die, election that the party will face sometime in the next year.

Much darker results of CCHQ's approach can be found in the suicide of Jade Smith and its treatment of allegations she made to the party, both of bullying within the local party and even more serious allegations of sexual abuse, and prior knowledge thereof. This is covered in the much greater detail it deserves elsewhere.

Jade definitely complained of the former to CCHQ and was not reassured by the response or treatment she received from them. She assured me that she would make a formal complaint about her allegation of prior knowledge of sexual abuse within the party but I was *never* contacted by CCHQ about that in my role as Chairman of South Tees.

When I subsequently approached CCHQ about the matter I was stonewalled and eventually ignored.

Given the seriousness of those allegations and the party's promise of an investigation into the other allegations Jade tweeted posthumously on her suicide in October 2019, the fact that to my knowledge no investigations were ever made speaks volumes about the nature of CCHQ. Whether this inaction was due to incompetence or a coverup I'll let you decide. Neither option speaks highly of the Conservative Party nor CCHQ.

Other 'highlights' of CCHQ's interesting administrative ways included never informing the association that our then Chairman, Malcolm Griffiths, had been suspended by the party for alleged Islamophobia, and that we were subsequently Chairman-less. We only heard this news from Malcolm himself and subsequently from The Guardian newspaper in its expose of about two dozen Tory councillors with questionable views, all of whom were suspended.

Maybe the welter of suspensions meant that an overworked and understaffed CCHQ never had the time to do us the courtesy of letting us know, but more likely it's a good example of the contempt the party nationally has for the activists in the regions who actually keep the whole show on the road.

This latter interpretation is supported by the fact that when the STCA Executive Council asked me, as acting Chairman and

Malcolm's successor, to write to CCHQ to ask for details of Malcolm's suspension, which I did, they never bothered to reply. Which was sadly par for the course.

When the Executive Council then asked for the association to raise concerns about Malcolm's treatment and also the fact we had never as an association been informed of the suspension of our Chairman, that letter also went unanswered.

Malcolm Griffiths had no real grounds for complaint about the fact of his suspension, however. Indeed, he admitted to me when I subsequently spoke to him about it, that if he had been the party's national Chairman he would not have hesitated to suspend himself either. In an expose by a twitter profile named 'Jacob'sFriends', apparently a backhanded and ironic fan club of Jacob Rees Mogg, a whole slew of Conservative councillors, former councillors and activists had been exposed for a range of dodgy social media pronouncements, ranging from the downright racist to the merely ill-judged.

Malcolm's transgressions were towards the higher end of alleged islamophobia within the party, and this was a red button topic back in 2019, though somewhat buried by the party and the media since. For the right wing press had been having a field day on the Corbyn Labour party's very real problem with anti-semitism and it was clear that Labour and the left wing press were determined to label the Tory party with a corresponding 'ism' or 'phobia' and Islamophobia was label they thought most likely to stick. Probably with good reason.

Ironically, one of the few examples of racism I had witnessed within the Tory party, several years prior, and on Tyneside, might best be ascribed to anti-semitism rather than islamophobia when an elderly member referred to a former business associate as a 'jew-boy', which took me aback at the time. I assumed at the time that there was no malice in the phrase as the member seemed quite fond of the acquaintance in question, but it's not a phrase I would have used. A generational thing perhaps.

More recently, the conflict in Gaza led one Conservative acquaintance to comment that the Israelis should be re-accommodated in Greenland as a solution to the conflict, which given their likely natural resistance to being moved raises the rather historically unpleasant spectre of forced deportations. A useful, but somewhat ironic reminder that anti-semitism is not a uniquely Labour problem.

But I digress, back to the actual allegation of prejudice we are dealing with.

Malcolm had a facebook habit, which for his age and otherwise lack of technological ability was quite impressive. He would sometimes post several times a day, on issues of political or current affairs interest mostly. Often he would post articles from online versions of the Telegraph or Times, on items which interested him and he would make a personal comment on it in his post. A bad habit he had also developed was to cull content from the article, especially if it was behind a paywall, and copy and paste it into his own post. Usually without attribution.

In the case of the post which got him suspended, he doubled down on this recklessness by quoting from an article featuring the Danish leader of Pegida, a rabidly anti muslim organisation, which was touching upon congenital abnormalities that occur within certain muslim communities who tend to practise marriages between cousins. The awful phrase 'inbreeding' made it from the article into Malcolm's facebook post and the die was cast.

Malcolm's foolishness was compounded by the fact that he had been warned about some of his posts, and that one in particular and advised to take it down. This warning I understand came from our own local MP, Simon Clarke. But the post stayed up and was later uncovered by Jacob's Friends and publicised in an article in the

Guardian that saw about two dozen Tory councillors immediately suspended by the party.

Malcolm complained to me that the issue of congenital abnormalities in muslim communities in Bradford, where cousin marriages are commonplace, had been the subject of a particular medical study in recent years which had in turn been reported in the Guardian itself, ironically enough. I explained to him that such issues *are* legitimate issues for discussion but he hadn't quoted the Guardian or the scientific study, but had instead directly used a quote from the virulently islamophobic leader of Pegida and a phrase that no sensible person should be repeating. He'd made this even worse by not attributing it, making it look like the expressions were entirely his own. As such I think he grudgingly accepted his eventual suspension from the party for a period of 12 months, and a requirement to attend diversity awareness training.

What Malcoolm didn't appreciate, and bringing us back to the topic of this chapter, the general incompetence of CCHQ, was the whole process by which he was suspended, which was long winded and shambolic.

What further rankled was that he was given no advice on accessing the required diversity training or how to go about rejoining the party once his suspension had been served. This in turn fed into the whole saga of the breakaway of rebel Tory councillors on Redcar and Cleveland Council who felt aggrieved for their colleague. So much so that they apparently continued to include Malcolm in their Conservative Group meetings despite his suspension, until they eventually jumped ship into the short-lived experiment that was the Cleveland Independent Group ('CIG' being entirely appropriate for Malcolm given his liking for hand-rolled fags)

The suspensions nationally were undoubtedly justified and necessary and helped to root out remaining racist and islamophobic attitudes among some Tory members and councillors that the article proved were still present.

For Islamophobia is undoubtedly an issue within the Conservative Party, as big names such as Baroness Warsi have publicised. Understandable alarm at radical islamism and a long series of terrorist plots in the UK and elsewhere, some successful and others thwarted, has mixed with an underlying suspicion of Islam and muslims, and intrinsic racism, in *some* members.

However, in fairness to the party, active measures have also been taken to identify and address such prejudice and put in measures to protect members from muslim background and provide avenues for redress when problems occur. These included a thorough review and consultation within the party conducted by one of the National Convention's Deputy Chairmen. Whether these measures are having much, or the desired effect, is however questionable.

However, In my time in the party I can't say I had come across much in the way of Islamophobia personally, though given I am non-muslim and that we had, to my knowledge, no muslim members locally, that is not surprising. Perhaps the lack of muslim members was itself an indication of Islamophobia? Or perhaps just a reflection of the fact in northern England, at least, that the muslim community's traditional political loyalties lie more naturally with the Labour Party.

The lack of black and asian members locally did cause me concern, though the fact that the majority of our membership came from the predominantly white rural parts of Teesside in East Cleveland perhaps gave some reasonable excuse for that. Nevertheless I was delighted to be instrumental in bringing onboard, as far as I'm aware, the first Asian Executive Council member in South Tees Conservatives' history, former Labour councillor Shamal Biswas The fact they were a former Labour councillor made it all the more satisfying!

The fact that Shamal is hindu, rather than muslim, is also perhaps an example of the strange drift of hindu voters towards the Tory

Party just as the Labour party had hoovered up Muslim votes for decades.

For all that the Conservative party locally, and for that matter nationally, is overwhelmingly white, middle-aged and middle-class there was a surprising lack of racism, *in my experience.* And whereas people from ethnic minority backgrounds experience the very real *overt* racism that definitely still clings on in British society, you have to be white to experience the more pernicious variety of *covert* racism that exists. For covert racists will say things in a group of wholly white people that they would never dream of saying in the presence of people from BAME backgrounds. If that acronym is still in favour? Hence white people are most likely to uncover covert racism.

But despite my many criticisms of the party in this book, rampant overt or even covert racism is not one of them. Maybe my experience is faulty in this, and I am sure examples of the grossest forms of racism do occur within the party (including the racist incidents detailed in an earlier chapter.) Such examples can be found out there with minimal research, but it never otherwise came across my personal radar.

Am I blind to this? I don't believe so as I've certainly come across and called out racism in other organisations and walks of life, so certainly can spot racism when it rears its ugly head. For I find racism grossly offensive on many fronts but not least the sheer injustice and irrationality that underpins and flows from it. Treating anyone differently on the basis of skin colour is the height of both injustice AND irrationality, and both offend me about equally.

So whilst the party membership IS old, traditionalist, and conservative with a small c and big c (unsurprisingly), it is not, in my experience, afflicted by racism any more so than society as a whole. Whilst it is ageing rapidly, many of that older membership were actually young adults during the more permissive 1960s and their attitudes are surprisingly enlightened on issues of race, and perhaps even more surprisingly, sexuality. Certainly the number of openly gay MPs we ended up with in this region after 2019 would suggest the party is taking a more grown up approach to issues of race and sexuality than used to be the case.

The example of Rishi Sunak, who famously became the MP in our association's neighbouring constituency of Richmond, North Yorkshire, and went on to even bigger things (California most likely) is a useful case in point. Sadly I never had the pleasure of experiencing one of Rishi's legendary summer garden parties, footmen and all, that local members liked to tell me about, the covid lockdowns during my Chairmanship of South Tees putting paid to any chance of that at the time. And this book doing likewise going forward,

I do have it on good authority however, from a senior officer of that association, that when they were choosing a replacement for William Hague as their candidate in what is the safest Tory seat in the country, Rishi's place on the shortlist caused some consternation among some local members. For some, his lack of connection to the area, or even the North generally, plus his lack of experience of rural life in just about the most rural constituency in England were black marks (no pun intended) against his chances. Some of that hesitancy, at least, would have been consciously, or subconsciously, based upon race and racism.

However, once wowed by his performance at the selection meetings, his polish, grasp of detail and, no doubt, merchant banker background, personal millions and good marriage to an even wealthier wife, were certainly enough to put to bed any doubts about his suitability which were grounded at least in part on his race. My source recounted how one of the fiercest critics of Rishi's inclusion on the shortlist, was instantly transformed into his most ardent admirer upon meeting the man in person. Dishy Rishi indeed.

Having said that, it is clear that there is a section of the party membership, and MPs, that is deeply antagonistic to Sunak, and his race undoubtedly plays a part in that. Both die-hard Boris fans and those from ukippy backgrounds find it hard to stomach Rishi as PM, and the oft used image of him as a snake covers both the alleged betrayal of his resignation from Johnson's government, and reflects racist sentiment about his heritage.

In truth though, most Conservatives are pragmatists, and pragmatists also most impressed by wealth and power, far more so than piffling matters such as skin colour. The colour of your old-school tie is more likely to affect their judgement of you, than the colour of your skin but that's a whole other matter.

Having said all the above, there is of course the chance that racist opinions have not faded away, but that they have simply become more guarded. Even racists are nowadays well aware of what opinions will be tolerated in polite company, and what opinions will not, so maybe some out and out racists are still there within the party, they are just being on their best behaviour.

The only real examples of racist attitudes I came across in my time at South Tees was racism hidden behind cloaking issues such as migration and foreign aid. Certainly some of the emails we received in the office about the small boats reeked of racism, ironically from elderly members least likely to be affected by an influx of arrivals across the channel. Another local member had an unhealthy obsession with cutting foreign aid, which seemed to crop up in almost every conversation, and I'm not convinced that pre-occupation was entirely fiscal.

Whether the influx of former Ukip members into the party post 2016 and the EU referendum will change these attitudes within the party is yet to be seen. Certainly the party leadership's preoccupation with 'stopping the small boats', Rwanda and 'culture wars' suggests that they are now chasing a different type of vote to the traditional Conservative one. A vote perhaps now more likely to follow types such as Lee Anderson out of the party and into the clutches of Reform UK

This chasing of hard right votes is only likely to get worse if, as expected, the Tories lose the next general election and the party membership swings to the hard right in a deluded mirror image of Labour members plumping for Jeremy Corbyn after their 2015 defeat.

If in doing so, the Conservative Party alienates its more traditional supporters on the centre-right it may well signal a terminal, but deserved, decline for the party.

Chapter 13 - Hubris: The Conservative Plan to Conquer North East England

Ambition is a great thing. I'm all for it, though arguably lacking it myself.

Yes, ambition is wonderful, but it does have to be realistic, grounded in fact and informed by the actual conditions prevailing at the time.

We'd all like to be superheroes, able to levitate and fly at will around the planet, fighting super-villains and spreading justice, goodwill and Conservative values wherever we ventured. But gravity is a thing. And political gravity is also a thing.

The Conservative Party's success in the December 2019 general election, especially in winning former 'Red Wall' seats that had been Labour for generations, seems to have sparked some rather fantastical, superhero thinking at CCHQ, far away in London. Party staff weren't literally donning capes and brightly coloured lycra to take the good fight for Conservative values even further into Labour's supervillain lair, but at times that kind of thinking seemed to have taken hold.

As discussed elsewhere, Conservative Campaign HeadQuarters seemed to have an uncanny knack of fighting the wrong election at the wrong time. Following modest success in winning the 2015 general election and giving David Cameron an unexpected working majority, by 2017 the polls suggested that Theresa May's Conservatives could wipe the floor with Jeremy Corbyn's Labour Party. As a result CCHQ plotted a remarkably expansive campaign, targeting seats in the North of England that had been staunchly Labour for quite some time, including launching the entire ill-fated 2017 campaign in the Labour heartland in Halifax. The resulting loss of May's majority would have far reaching effects for her, delivering Brexit and getting pretty much anything of worth through the House of Commons.

By contrast, in autumn 2019 and no doubt with fingers still singed from the 2017 experience, CCHQ had tight control over what they regarded as the winnable target seats that would get Boris Johnson returned with a workable majority. To the extent that those seats regarded as 'unwinnable' might as well not have existed. (In some cases they didn't appear to be on CCHQ's radar at all: read my experience about Redcar constituency in the chapter on CCHQ)

Any venturing outside of this 'target seat' plan was strictly discouraged, with the CCHQ Candidates Team's control over candidates' futures fully deployed to keep those regarded as standing in unwinnable seats on the straight and narrow and working instead for the election of colleagues in the identified 'winnable seats' nearby.

Here in North East England the boots on the ground became increasingly convinced that far more seats were in play than the campaign bods in London had in mind, and candidates and associations chafed at the controls imposed from the centre.

Here in South Tees the association funded a full second leaflet for Jacob Young in Redcar, in addition to the mandatory election address that all candidates are allowed for free delivery by the Royal Mail. This was in part, at least, done at the encouragement of Simon Clarke, our sitting MP in neighbouring Middlesbrough South and East Cleveland, whose fondness for following electoral forecasts on the website 'Electoral Calculus on an almost hourly basis had convinced was a viable target. In fairness to Simon, and as you know I do always try to be fair to people (it's a major weakness!) this was a pretty selfless act, although our backing of his campaign was so overwhelming that we could afford to divert a few resources to Jacob's campaign in Redcar.

In fairness to Jacob (there I go again) he also funded part of his second campaign leaflet and delivery out of his own funds. This decision turned out to be a good thing, as by many accounts the postal election address remained largely undelivered right up until polling day, having been massively delayed by being well down the list of what CCHQ deemed priority material at the party's contracted printers.

At the North East Regional Conference, November 2019, held at the Ramside Hall Hotel outside Durham, activists from various north east constituencies railed against the controls imposed from London and the perceived lack of ambition being shown. Confusion at which candidates had been appointed for potentially winnable seats was widespread, including the Sedgefield constituency once held by Tony Blair. In a fast moving situation early in the campaign the overwhelming feeling was that the party was lacking ambition and playing far too defensive a game.

And so it proved. The results in 2019 showed that yet again the party 'experts' at CCHQ in London had fought the wrong campaign at the wrong time. Though such was the landslide result, because of the very real desire to get Brexit done and the wholesale rejection of Jeremy Corbyn by traditional Labour voters, that the damage done was only to egos at CCHQ rather than the government's majority.

Which brings us to the Conservative Party's grand plan to build on this success and conquer even more territory in Labour's northern heartland, which from the perspective of 2024 and a Tory party facing electoral oblivion instead, does rather smack of super-hero thinking. Or hubris, if you prefer.

This plan entailed a much more centralised approach to campaigning in the North East. Instead of party campaign managers attached to individual target constituencies or Federations such as STCA, managing campaigns at a local level and working closely with candidates and local volunteers, all campaign managers in the region would work out of a central office. A grand, shiny new office. A physical office in a bricks and mortar building rather than the virtual office that just about every other organisation in the world was moving towards, post pandemic.

This Regional Campaign Office would be in a theoretical gleaming new office building in Washington (Tyne and Wear, not DC, though the suspicions of those of us in the south of the region was that it might as well have been District of Columbia, given the likely attention we would receive from such a team.)

For the suspicion was that once comfortably ensconced in just such an office the attraction of driving for over an hour and something like 60 miles to the wilds of East Cleveland on the very edge of the region would be easy to resist. The fear was that especially in the post-covid world of Zoom and Teams meetings, instructions would be issued by such virtual meetings, email and whatsapp messages and any physical presence on the ground would be rare indeed.

This fear was shared by all those Conservative Party associations and their Officers in the south of the region, which just happened to be the very associations with actual, existing, real, Conservative MPs. The self-same ones elected in 2019.

To those of us who had enjoyed unexpected success in 2019 and now had Conservative MPs, often for the first time in years, if not ever, the suspicion was that defending those seats was now playing second best to making speculative gains in the north of the region, where the shiny new office was to be based. In effect risking actual MPs, in pursuit of imaginary ones.

This fear was reinforced when the proposal document showed a clear concentration on the centre and north of the region, in particular Tyne and Wear. It was remarkably confirmed, jaw-droppingly so, when a senior figure within the party, and one offering to find funding for the entire proposal, stated at the meeting what the extraordinary objective of the whole plan was. This party figure was Sir John Hall.

Now Sir John Hall is a great man, without doubt. And a great businessman, without doubt, who transformed retail, and arguably economic fortunes generally, in the region with his MetroCentre creation in the 1980s. A great Geordie, no doubt at all, given his previous ownership and nurturing of Newcastle United during the 1990s.

A great man indeed. You'll get no argument from me on that, for I hold the man in the highest possible regard.

But an abysmal political strategist if this revelation was anything to go by.

For the objective of this North East Campaign Team strategy, according to Sir John, was for the Conservative Party to take control of Newcastle City Council.

Now, I've lived on Tyneside, and know the area, its politics and its people well. I have the highest regard and affection for an area I regard as being one of several adopted homes I've made down the years (for I seem to be a bit of a wanderer)

Specifically I spent eight happy years residing in the People's Socialist Republic of Gateshead, and several of those years fruitlessly trying to persuade the good people of that area to vote Conservative. The appetite for doing so is adequately reflected by the fact that the last Conservative councillor in Gateshead had been Martin, now Lord, Callanan in the early 1990s.

Newcastle likewise had not had a single Conservative councillor in many a moon, and the biggest impact any Conservative politician had had in Newcastle in recent years was a penny-pinching appearance (also unsuccessful) of a local Tory activist on Channel Four's 'Come Dine With Me'. Pigs trotters, I believe, were on the menu. Like the Conservatives on Tyneside, an acquired taste.

As I say, ambition is a great thing. But ludicrous ambition for fantastically speculative gains, that runs the risk of causing very real damage to what you already have, is just plain stupid. An MP in your hand is worth two in the bush, so to speak. This was super-hero thinking that wasn't super at all.

To set the scene for the showdown over these plans I must take you back to winter 2021 and the quaint surroundings of Benton Conservative Club, a faded edifice paying homage to a previous glorious past of the party on Tyneside. Like some dreary High Noon, association officers and officials from across the region had been called together to discuss the CCHQ master plan for conquest of the North East.

The building had seen better days, with faded furniture and teetering tables scattered somewhat haphazardly around a tired, and rather cold, club room. To add insult to injury for those dragged up the A19 on a cold Saturday morning, for a meeting on a plan they all found ludicrous and dangerous in equal measure, refreshments had to be paid for.

The CCHQ Regional Campaign manager, who did actually live close to the North East, though on the opposite side of the Pennines, gave an uninspiring presentation on the proposal document we had all previously been supplied with and had a chance to comment on. Neville Lishman, for that was his name, is not a natural salesman, though it's doubtful Arthur Daley or Delboy Trotter could have done a better job of selling such shoddy goods as the proposal as it stood.

Although those attendees from the north of the region were generally in favour of the prospect of getting more campaign attention from the party, neglected as they had been for many years, if not decades, those officers from the south of the region were overwhelmingly against. Not to say aghast.

For those of us with MPs not only had the most to lose in terms of their tenure in parliament, under the plans we would be expected to fork out more than associations without MPs. In the case of a federation such as STCA, lucky enough to have won two Tory MPs at the last election, largely down to our own efforts and with little thanks to a negative CCHQ, we would be expected to fork out £6000 a year for this grand scheme. Two lots of £3000 per MP, which not only created a perverse incentive NOT to win too many MPs in your federation, but also represented two times what we had paid for the full-time services of a dedicated Campaign Manager for the last few years. And all for just a *share* in a campaign team settled in a shiny new office miles away in Washington, Tyne and Wear.

All in all, the proposal was about as appealing as a bucket of warm sick to those of us from the south of the region, and we said as much, picking holes in the plans, from the office's location, to its funding, to its overall strategy, which was flawed, to say the least.

I pointed out the perverse incentive the funding formula made, the likelihood that we would seldom see much of any of the campaign team on the ground, working with the volunteers who actually win elections. Not least when campaign managers travel expenses and travelling time had to be accounted for during elections, all counting towards the overall, often tight, spending limits imposed on candidates by the Electoral Commission.

For good measure I threw in my view that any physical office was a questionable necessity at all in these modern, post covid days. Times where any good campaign manager would regard their smartphone and laptop as their office. Not to mention their car, which had the additional advantage of being mobile and not rooted to the ground in Washington, miles from the actual battleground seats that would decide the next election.

Through all these objections I noticed Sir John slumping ever further down into his seat, head occasionally in his hands, which would rub wearily at his forehead, seemingly in frustration and incredulity at the objections being raised by these obvious idiots from the south of the region, outside his beloved Tyneside. We clearly couldn't understand the grand strategy that would deliver his homeland safely into the hands of the Conservative Party and out of the decades long bondage of Labour one-party rule. Worse than that we were showing ourselves as ungrateful for the lion's share of funding he was offering to generate from his business and social contacts. We were clearly buffoons.

To lighten the mood I offered up my final objection that as a tight-fisted Yorkshireman I would naturally be against my association spending any more money on any new plan, no matter its merits. This raised a genuine laugh in an otherwise dour meeting but I noticed that Sir John wasn't laughing.

I parted company with the Conservative Party a few months later, as you're aware, due to my failure to even be offered an assessment centre for the party's parliamentary candidates list, despite the three years of hard work and stress undertaken for the party for no reward whatsoever, and detailed in this tome.

I don't know whether my objections to the grand strategy of the North East Campaign Team were held against me in my application; other reasons were eventually given for the failure of my application, though it's clear that the party values 'yes men' over those who actually voice an opinion, and who take their duty to their local associations and members seriously.

As for the plan itself, it really does appear like genuinely magical thinking from the perspective of early 2024, as the Conservative Party reaches back into its traditional heartland in seeking to avoid a projected existential drubbing at the polls.

There are those in the party who still believe that northern Red Wall voters are there for the taking, harbouring as they do naturally socially conservative views that the party can tap into through 'culture wars', being 'anti-woke' and banging on about the perils of asylum backlogs and mass migration. Mass migration and asylum backlogs the party itself has presided over.

Many of those clinging on to these beliefs do so in the desperate hope of also clinging onto their previously Red Wall seats in the very North East of England that under the plan was soon to be a hotbed of Conservative rule.

In a cost of living crisis that has seen many in this region genuinely fear for their futures and those of their families, and who have witnessed collapsing public services, from crumbling schools to never ending NHS queues, the likelihood of such northern voters being wooed by the authors of those calamities, by a promise of old-fashioned values, seem slim indeed.

Chances are that the Conservative Party will need genuine superheroes if the hopes of a new renaissance in the North are to be fulfilled.

Or a miracle.

Chapter 14 - Councillors are Revolting

(In a recent development: Cllr Vera Rider, whose behaviour is detailed below, behaviour which led to her being thrown out of the Conservative Party for 4 years in 2021, has as of November 2023, been readmitted as a Conservative councillor on Redcar and Cleveland Council. I'll let you judge just how desperate the party must be to do so, as you read about the chaos she caused, which led to her being thrown out in the first place.)

Revolting.

Now, not all of them, obviously. I've known many very decent, honourable and hard-working councillors who are great advocates and activists for their local communities, and who play a vital role in our democracy and public life. They include those from all political parties and the many independents who now also populate local government.

Others, in my experience, however, have been grifters, lazy, petty, motivated by delusions of grandeur, and in some cases borderline lunatic.

More on that later, but 'revolting' of course can have a different meaning as well, and it's in that sense of the word; 'rebellious, renegade , breaking-away', that this chapter will proceed. Though in some cases there is, in my view, a large amount of cross-over between the two meanings.

The 'revolting councillors' I'm specifically thinking of here are the half dozen or so Conservative Councillors on Redcar & Cleveland Council who revolted against the local party in 2021 and formed a breakaway group: the Cleveland Independent Group (or 'CIG' for short, which was a rather appropriate acronym for a bunch of local politicians at the fag-end of their careers)

I was Chairman of South Tees at the time and I must take some responsibility for the mess that unfolded. Indeed, I offered my resignation as Chairman to the party on at least two occasions (and to be honest its acceptance would have been a blessing) Though it was declined on each occasion.

It must be stated that Covid undoubtedly played its part in the debacle to follow, and that harmony in South Tees Conservatives (what there ever was of it) was one of the many victims of that dread disease. For the lockdowns which were imposed, and in which we were hunkered down when this mess kicked off and concluded, played their part in feeding paranoia and neuroses (always not far below the surface in politics anyway in my experience) and reducing the effective communication that good relations rely upon.

However, the origins of this breakaway go back far beyond both my involvement in South Tees or the coronavirus altogether, and are rooted in Brexit, the resulting mutual hatred between Tory Leavers and Tory Remainers, and the rather juvenile behaviour and miscalculations of one of our local Conservative MPs, erstwhile Cabinet Minister, Simon Clarke MP.

That's not to say that there wasn't fault on both sides: the CIG bunch had the morals of an ashtray ironically enough (in some cases) and were also motivated (in some cases again) by the rather venal attributes I mentioned at the start of the chapter. It's fair to say that few on either side (or the Conservative Party generally for that matter) come out of this saga with any credit, myself included, but it raises some interesting points about the state of our democracy, human nature, chaos theory, and the perils of clearing your Action Points from a committee meeting.

If I may start with the immediate cause of the rebellion and work backwards from there, I can also pitch this book as being one about time-travel. More seriously, though, it is probably the best, if anti-chronological, way to go about it.

The final straw in this saga of party in-fighting seems to have been the Redcar & Cleveland Council Longbeck Ward by-election in May 2021 and my suggestion that the association should request a supportive quote for our candidate's leaflet from the sitting Conservative Councillor Vera Rider.

Vera was one of two councillors in the ward, the actual vacancy having come about from the sad death of long-term Tory councillor Nora Cooney. I felt that such a request was a common courtesy to a sitting councillor, and not to have asked would have been, well, rude.

Vera was also an STCA Executive Council member, the body that governs the association alongside elected party officers such as myself and therefore heavily involved in all decisions about the association's direction and specifically dealing with the ever thorny issue of non-payment of the Councillor's campaign levy (more on this later)

The combined issues of non-payment of the levy and an endorsement for the party's candidate (plus the linked issue of councillor's newsletters generally) would be the final straw leading to the breakaway of the CIG councillors, and allegations against myself of intimidation and bullying. I'll let you, the reader, be the judge of which direction the intimidation and bullying came from in the following exchanges.

As mentioned, I made the suggestion of asking for a supportive quote as a courtesy to Vera, as I felt it would be discourteous not to ask a sitting Tory councillor for a quote for the campaign leaflet of the party candidate hoping to become her colleague in the same ward. Looking back, I suspect the rebels regarded this as a rather Machiavellian ploy by me to test loyalties and stir up trouble, given the now obvious ill-feeling between Councillor Rider and the Turners, Steve and Andrea (Steve being a former council colleague of Vera in the same ward and Andrea being the current candidate.)

I only wish I could lay claim to such cunning, as it was actually a genuine request made for genuine reasons and I personally had nothing to gain from exacerbating the tensions already present in the local party. That and the fact I'm far too lazy to engage in party intrigue. Hence why I'm sitting here writing this tome, rather than drawing a salary as an elected politician.

It is true that I was aware of some apparent ill-will between Cllr Rider and Steve Turner, our soon to be Police and Crime Commissioner, one-time Longbeck councillor and husband of the current candidate, Andrea Turner.

Some time earlier whilst encouraging local councillors to provide the party with content for newsletters for their wards (like pulling teeth in most cases) I had mentioned to Vera that it would be good (and would provide much-needed content) if ward newsletters could also feature other local Conservative politicians, like our MPs, our local Mayor, and our PCC candidate. A way of putting forward the positive 'Conservative Team' identity I was so keen to pursue in a region previously lacking that many Tory representatives.

Vera replied, rather pointedly, that she was happy to feature "Jacob and Ben" (Redcar Tory MP Jacob Young and Tees Valley Mayor Ben Houchen) on her leaflets, but no mention of Steve Turner, our PCC candidate.

I later asked Steve Turner if there was ill-will between him and Vera from his time as a fellow Longbeck councillor, first Ukip and then Tory. He said he couldn't think of anything in particular but that they moved in different circles and that some of Vera's crowd might not be keen on him, or words to that effect. This turned out to be monumental under-statement.

Vera was also undoubtedly not happy that Andrea Turner had won the nomination for the Longbeck contest over her favoured candidate, a friend who lived in the ward, whilst Andrea did not (she lived in a neighbouring ward that used to be part of Longbeck prior to boundary changes, so was still pretty much as local as local can be.)

Vera was also no doubt irate that she had failed to gain entry to the initial selection process for the ward, held online due to covid, and administered by one of our deputy chairmen. This initial vote was meant to be attended by Conservative Party members who lived in the ward, who had all received invites by email. About half an hour after the meeting had commenced with the grand total of zero members in attendance, and ten minutes after it had therefore been closed, I received an angry email from Vera stating she had not been granted entry.

After much to-ing and fro-ing by email it transpired she had not clicked a link to pre register, as required under party rules, and therefore hadn't been sent the link to actually gain entry to the meeting. The rules *were* a palaver, and probably more suited to the Home Counties where party membership isn't limited to one man and his dog, as in these parts, but rules is rules, as they say. And I am a stickler.

As it happens, Vera's failure to read her emails properly, though a concerning feature for a sitting borough councillor, made not a jot of difference to the result of the vote. As the minimum required 15 members in the ward had not turned up (did we actually have 15 members in the ward?) the decision wouldn't have been binding anyway and would fall to the selection panel instead, upon which Vera sat and had a vote anyway. These things clearly rankled though, as did the panel's eventual choice of Andrea Turner.

The local party selection process had, therefore, been entirely above-board, fair and in line with the Conservative Party's labyrinthine Covid selection rules. As Chairman, one reason I insisted the association followed all such rules to the letter (unlike my predecessor's apparently more freestyle approach) was the as-it-turned-out vain hope that doing so would avoid conflict.

(By way of full disclosure, I was also a candidate in that selection meeting, and had accidentally been denied a vote which I should have had under party rules, my deputy not letting me back into the Zoom meeting in time as I had sat out the other candidate's interviews, again in line with party rules. I had let the oversight go and not even mentioned it, other than to my deputy, to avoid embarrassing him (a thoroughly good chap) and been happy to accept Andrea as actually the best candidate for the by-election)

So, there *were* reasons to suspect Vera was not entirely enamoured of the party's candidate for the vacancy in her ward but my suggestion we ask her for a quote was made entirely in good faith. Honest.

When we received a quote from Vera that pointedly didn't even mention the party, or its candidate, let alone say anything positive about either of them, I asked my Deputy Chairman Political, who was handling the leaflet, to get back to Vera and ask her to say something positive that we could actually use.

I take the view that *everything* on a campaign leaflet, literally *everything:* text, logos, pictures, graphics etc, should serve the purpose of persuading voters to vote for your party and your candidate, or else it shouldn't be there. The sad reality is that most leaflets are glanced at by most voters on the way to the bin, so every inch of leaflet space should be utilised to persuade voters to vote, and to vote for you. Anything else is, quite literally, waste.

The only conclusion most voters could have drawn from Vera's offered quote was that there must be ill-feeling in the local Conservative Party (they'd have been right) given Vera's rather chilly non-endorsement of either the party or its candidate.

Unfortunately my deputy instead proposed a form of words to Vera that could be used as a quote. I wouldn't have done so, I would have asked her for her own quote but with a bit more positivity. As it was, the approach was like a red rag to a heifer in a Teesside china shop, and the reaction was explosive.

When it all kicked off I was enjoying a lazy lie-in in bed (Churchill did his best work there, and rather fittingly a war was about to start. Though unlike Boris, I'm not drawing comparisons with the great man.)

There followed the proceeding email exchange (typos, spelling mistakes and grammatical errors have not been corrected, nor has 'sic' been deployed, it would take too long)

18 February 2021 (Email from me as Chairman to all STCA Councillors on behalf of the STCA Executive - as an STCA Executive Council member, Vera had already had sight of this for comment or objection, as had all Executive Council members. The content was agreed by the Executive Council as it had been circulated beforehand without objection. I'm nothing if not 'collegiate'. Or possibly just eejit.)

"South Tees Conservative Councillors

Dear Colleagues

Late last year I contacted you on behalf of the STCA Executive to detail the help that STCA can offer to councillors and the assistance we hope for in return. Despite the very difficult circumstances imposed by Covid there is now hope that a return to normal life is on the horizon and so I wanted to follow up on that email.

We face two vital by-elections in May which we hope will strengthen the Conservative Group on RCBC and naturally most of our effort will concentrate on those contests for the time being. However, we still intend to support those councillors who pay the levy with producing and financing newsletters this year when restrictions allow. To that end, I'd be grateful if councillors could give some thought to suitable content for newsletters.

For those councillors who do not pay the levy it is still a requirement of STCA and the party that they maintain communications with their ward residents in the form of regular newsletters. Once restrictions allow, we would expect a minimum of three ward newsletters per year to be produced, financed and delivered by those councillors.

Please note that to protect both yourselves and the party ALL such newsletters or leaflets should be checked over by STCA prior to printing to avoid potential legal issues."

Future Plans

STCA is also developing plans for the next full round of elections in 2023, to identify target wards and potential candidates, with the aim of being in joint control of RCBC and holding the balance of power on Middlesbrough Council.

It would help our planning if sitting councillors could advise us of their intention to run again in 2023, or not if that is the case.

Under party rules, re-selection is not automatic and sitting councillors will need to show that they have been performing the role of councillor to the required standard throughout their terms. Evidence of this will be helpful in the re-selection process and I urge colleagues to keep a record of work undertaken and successes achieved.

Despite the very difficult times we are living through, STCA is keen to plan for a better future and to ensure that our local councillors play a strong role in that. Please do get in touch with any queries or suggestions.

Best regards

Lee R Holmes
STCA Chairman on behalf of the STCA Executive"

Vera's Response February 19 9.30am

"Is it actually a legal requirement that councillors who pay for their own newsletters have to have them checked by the S T.C.A ?"

You'll note the lack of pleasantries. This is how the email was sent and received, no editing, as with all other emails quoted.

Even in these impersonal, modern times, in sending an email it is still usual, not to mention polite, to address the recipient, and I would make clear at this point that I was at the time on first-name terms with all our Executive Council members and Borough councillors, Vera included. Hence my response, despite Vera's rather terse opening, was somewhat more polite:

February 19 10.19am

"Hello Vera

If a newsletter is going out in the name of the Conservative Party then the party needs to make sure that its content doesn't damage the reputation of the party.

It's also to protect the councillors as there are strict legal requirements laid down by the Electoral Commission regarding the imprint etc.

Finally the party pays for electoral insurance which helps to protect our councillors against legal action resulting from electioneering etc. This certainly won't apply if content is not being reviewed by the party to avoid potential legal difficulties.

So this requirement is as much about protecting councillors as it is about protecting the party

Lee."

All true, by the way, though perhaps particularly relevant to Cllr Rider who had a record of being a bit of a loose cannon when it came to media pronouncements, for example her very negative spin on Simon Clarke's resignation detailed earlier.

Vera's reply February 19 10 10.41am

"In that case you will make sure that the piece I sent you for Andrea's leaflet goes in rather than the one you wrote for me to which I did not agree
For clarification I am copying Philip in to this email"

Some might regard this as a tad aggressive. Demanding even. Still rather rude in the failure to address the recipient as well. For the record, I hadn't written anything for Vera, my Deputy was dealing with the leaflet, but the small matter of facts often didn't seem to matter. Philip is Councillor Philip Thomson, the then head of the Conservative Group on RCBC.

My reply February 19 10.49am

"Hello Vera

With regard to the endorsement of Andrea as the party's candidate we have requested from you for Andrea's leaflet, in my opinion your suggested statement is not sufficient.

Your statement pointedly does not actually endorse Andrea. It doesn't even mention her by name. Nor does it even offer support to the party or the party's candidate generally.

Vera, you are the sitting CONSERVATIVE PARTY councillor for Longbeck ward and in my opinion the party is not asking too much of you to endorse the Conservative Party candidate for the same ward by name.

I would hope that Philip, as Conservative Group leader, would be of the same opinion. We are after all spending STCA money trying to get another Conservative party councillor elected.

Lee ."

Vera's response February 19 11.41am

"I think it is sufficient and you will put that in. I do not know Andrea Turner so my statement is correct and not yours you do not need to remind me I am a conservative councillor. I work hard and tirelessly for my community and can i also remind you that while in lockdown and I couldn't deliver ny leaflets, I still continued to pay my levy . Dont threaten me because if you go down that road you will regret it .

It is a disgrace the way you dictate to elected members so remember that"

Hmmmmmm. Interesting response: "you will put that in", "you will regret it" and "so remember that." Some may view this email from Vera as bullying and dictating, the very accusation she later made against me, but I'm not one to complain! It is amusing that she is accusing ME of dictating to councillors, in rather dictatorial fashion.

Interestingly Councillor Rider was emailing from her official Redcar and Cleveland Council email account and was arguably in breach of the council's own Code of Conduct for councillors in making such threats. I did consider making a complaint against Vera under the Code but didn't, as I'm not actually the vindictive type. Despite the impression this book may be giving!

My reply February 2019 12.06pm, now slightly exasperated, not just with Vera but with the whole poisonous nature of local Conservative party infighting at South Tees. (I would add that the CAPITALS are not meant to be SHOUTING but merely used for emphasis given the difficulty in using italics on gmail on my mobile phone):

"Vera

I am not threatening anyone or dictating anything and find your assertions deeply offensive.

Quite frankly, I am sick and tired of dealing with the nonsense thrown up by this association, not least you.

You are not only an elected CONSERVATIVE councillor but an STCA Executive member and one might hope, as such, you would want to support both the association and your fellow Conservative candidates.

What Ron Armstrong is trying to do as Deputy Chairman Political is to get another Conservative Councillor elected in Longbeck ward. He can do without wasting time on your nonsense in refusing to endorse the party's chosen candidate.

We have asked you as the sitting councillor (AS A COURTESY TO YOU) if you would like to provide a brief statement endorsing the party's candidate. Your statement doesn't do that:

"

Vera Rider, sitting Councillor for Longbeck Ward, (Vera)

has welcomed this by-election, delayed by Covid-19,

as the opportunity of having another elected member

to support her work on Redcar & Cleveland Council.

The Ward needs two hard working representatives which had **been the case prior to the sad passing of Councillor Norah Cooney, who had served the Ward through its continued development over four decades."**

It pointedly fails to endorse Andrea as the Conservative Party candidate and will not be used. If it is all you are willing to say then we will do without your 'endorsement' altogether but what a disgraceful way for a Conservative councillor and STCA Executive member to behave.

Lee R Holmes
STCA Chairman"

It's worth noting that the quote originally offered by Vera Rider had 'Vera' in brackets and red coloured font. Perhaps evidence that somebody else had had a hand in drafting the quote from 'Vera'. It seems the disgruntled Tory councillors on RCBC may have been working together to stir things up at this stage. At this point, Vera mysteriously breaks off this email chain to continue in a brand new email thread, which she copies in to other RCBC Conservative councillors. The suspiciously minded among us might think this was a way of editing the email exchange so far, to remove her rather aggressive tone from the view of her fellow councillors, and make me look the aggressor.

Vera's reply in the new thread February 19 12.13pm

"RE: South Tees Conservative Councillors

And I am really tired of you and your dictatorial attitude

I hope you see the error of your ways and either put in what I sent you or leave it out altogether.
I will NOT tolerate bullying by you or anyone"

Ah, the 'B' word. Bullying has become a big issue in modern life, it can destroy people and is rightly regarded as very serious. However, false allegations of bullying can also destroy people. It's fair to say my patience and emolience had run out at this point.

My reply, in the new thread, February 19 12.19pm

"Right that's it.

I am not going to be baselessly accused of bullying by you, or anybody else.

Nowhere in this email exchange have I threatened, or dictated, or bullied.

Either withdraw that accusation and apologise for it, or provide evidence of where I have bullied you, or I will refer this entire matter to the Executive for their adjudication.

Lee R Holmes
STCA Chairman"

Vera's reply, copying in the entire Conservative councillor group

"Good idea

I think the whole Cobservatice Group should see these emails so I am am copying them all I"

At this point, Cllr Graham Jeffery, replies to Vera's copied emails (seemingly unaware he was also replying to me. Cllr Jeffery was one of the worst offenders in refusing to pay the campaign levy that ALL Conservative council candidates agree to in order to be selected as candidates. Vera *had been* a payer and adamant that other non-payers must be made to pay, but after a chat with Cllr Jeffery had mysteriously changed her mind.

Cllr Graham Jeffery February 19 12.28

"Dear Vera

I am discussed by this man's attitude.

I am still waiting for answers on the threat to deselect if the levy is not paid!!

Graham"

My response February 19 12.33pm

"Dear Cllr Jeffery

Nowhere in my email to Conservative Group Councillors does it threaten deselection for non payment of the Levy.

I have not received a reply from you so am bemused as to how you are awaiting a reply from me, but I am happy to answer any queries on behalf of the STCA Executive who agreed the content of the original email to councillors.

Best regards

Lee R Holmes
STCA Chairman"

Cllr Jeffery didn't respond and it seems some councillors' honesty is matched only by their reading and writing skills. Cllr Jeffery is now a LibDem councillor, and I can only hope that they have more luck in getting him to pay towards their campaign funds than we had.

Looking back, these exchanges do have a bit of the flavour of the infamous Handforth Parish Council massacre that became such a hit on Youtube, also a product of covid mania. Sadly, unlike Jackie Weaver, I had no mute button.

From there the whole sorry saga snowballed, and reams of emails were sent and received as I reported the whole affair, and specifically the allegation of bullying made against me by Cllr Rider, both to the Executive Council and the party at regional level.

The allegation of bullying was as baseless as these emails make clear, and was dismissed by the party locally and nationally. But the damage to me personally stood.

False allegations cause harm and I bear the psychological scars of dealing with some councillors whose unreasonableness verges on the pathological. (It should be noted that all the councillors in the CIG faction were later thrown out of the Conservative Party following the prescribed disciplinary process chaired by an independent chairman. The fact that at least one of them has now been readmitted shows that the Conservative Party is as cynical as it is desperate, and places short term political gain above standards of behaviour, decency and the truth)

The faction composed of Cllrs Philip Thomson, Vera Rider, Graham Jeffery and Cliff Foggo decided upon breaking away as the 'CIGs' and trying to persuade other Conservative councillors to do the same, with no success. Each had personal motives for doing so, beyond Vera Rider's vitriolic allegations or the other wider political factors of note that played a part in the revolt.

They were also joined by my predecessor as Chairman, Malcolm Griffiths, who had in 2019 been thrown out of the party nationally due to his ill-judged facebook comments. I understand he had still been attending Conservative Group meetings despite this.

For Philip Thomson, the Conservative Group Leader on RCBC, motives for this breakaway stretched back into the brexit issue, personal animosity between him and/or some of his local volunteers and Simon Clarke MP (arising from brexit) and an apparent, rather clumsy, attempt to replace him as group leader by another councillor apparently with the support of Simon Clarke.

I probably hadn't enamoured myself with Philip by *privately* suggesting to him that I hoped he would have the best interests of the group at heart in deciding how long he would stay on as group leader.

This was a diplomatic way of suggesting to him that he wasn't the best person for the role, being perhaps the most tedious man alive, one who struggled to communicate with both his own councillors and the voting public. I'm sure this opinion was also shared by Simon Clarke in his cack-handed involvement in trying to unseat

Philip as group leader, though we never discussed the matter together.

Philip had also recently had his nose put out of joint by being pulled up for making misleading statements to the Executive Council of STCA (Philip was also a member) on a matter of local political controversy. Philip was adamant that he had misspoken accidentally and I accepted his explanation, and turned down a demand for an apology from Philip made by another Executive Council member. Ever the peacemaker.

Although I accepted Philip's explanation by way of drawing a line under the matter and avoiding further ill-will in the local party, the background to the issue showed a pattern of evasiveness by Philip that suggests his misstatements might not have been entirely accidental.

The issue arose from news reports on a planned Council Tax rise by the Independent-LibDem coalition that ran RCBC and whether the Tory group would support the plans. In a facebook exchange another member asserted that the Tory group had already voted to support a rise (it was mistakenly referring to the previous year when such support HAD been given)

Another member of the Executive Council then emailed me to ask if this was true and made the not unreasonable point that Conservative council candidates had run on a platform of a Council Tax freeze in 2019, so didn't it then look dishonest to back a Council Tax rise in the following year? Not having been party to any of these decisions I suggested that they raise the issue with Philip as Conservative Group Leader. The member did so and copied me into the email exchange.

I have to say that Philip's replies seemed evasive and he didn't actually answer the points raised, despite several emails from the member concerned. The email exchange seemed to peter out and I assumed the matter had been dropped. Now, how does that saying about 'assume' go? For the issue was not dead, but raised in Any Other Business at the end of the next Executive Council meeting. A dangerous thing is 'AOB'.

Philip appeared flustered to have the issue raised (and indeed complained later that he felt the question had been hostile to him) but his explanation of how the leaflets put out by candidates didn't actually reflect the group manifesto in 2019, and that he had not been party to the leaflets drawn up by the local MP and Campaign Manager seemed reasonable enough.

In addition, so did his and Vera's defence of the need for increased local government spending given constraints imposed by central government and the ever growing demands of an ageing population and the growing numbers of children in the care of the local authority. If he'd bothered to reply as such to the initial emails the whole issue could have been sorted before the meeting.

In doing so however, Philip asserted that the Conservative group had NOT voted for *any* Council Tax increase. This struck me as odd, as I was quite convinced the group had in the previous year voted in favour of an increase, but as Philip was generally usually very knowledgeable on all matters council related, and as it was at the end of a very long zoom meeting, I accepted his assurance with the comment that you 'can't believe everything you read on social media'.

Being a bit of a politics geek, and troubled by the sense that I must have misremembered on this issue, I did however check the record the next day and it was clear that the Conservative Group, under Philip's leadership *had* voted for a Council Tax increase in the previous year. It was a matter of public record.

I discussed this with my two deputy chairmen as the issue of being straight with other members of the Executive Council is an important one. We resolved that I should contact Philip and ask him to correct the record and correct his misstatement of fact.

Philip did so, grudgingly, but this undoubtedly contributed to the ill-will that in turn contributed to the breakaway. I suspect, aware of political paranoia as I am, that Philip may have thought this was some kind of set-up to embarrass him by the Clarke/Brexiteer faction in the local party (it wasn't, certainly as far as I'm aware, and I was not part of that faction) and in fairness, if Philip had deigned to answer a reasonable query put to him in the original email by a fellow Executive Council member, rather than stone-walling, he wouldn't have embarrassed himself at the meeting.

I happened to sympathise with the explanations given by Philip on how the leaflets contained promises never agreed by the council group at the behest of others like Simon Clarke, and sympathise with the difficult funding issues faced by all local councils, and certainly wasn't involved in any plot to embarrass him, for whatever reason. However, it's clear the poison already present in the local party was distilled further.

Philip's leading of the breakaway was particularly hurtful to me as I had been very open in a recent email to him about my wishes for the association and for better relations with councillors, who often seemed to feel themselves a breed apart in the local party. Sadly the candour and appeal for better team-spirit that I made in the following email reply to Philip (edited to remove irrelevant content) appears to have been ignored:

"Good morning Philip

I appreciate that you have clarified to me how you came to inadvertently mis-state the voting record of the group on Council Tax increases (and the information you have supplied is very useful in doing so)...

I'm surprised and disappointed that you regarded the atmosphere as 'hostile', there was certainly no hostility from me towards you.

In fact, I accepted your assurances on the matter (despite niggling doubts I had, but that I didn't want to raise at the end of an admittedly long meeting) I actually concluded matters by saying something about 'not believing everything you read on social media' which could have been taken as a criticism of the member for raising the issue.

I could be put-out that your misstatement of the facts has made ME look rather foolish and indeed I have contacted the member concerned to apologise for my comments.

For the record: the member raised this whole issue with me by email following another local members assertion on Facebook that local Tory Councillors voted in favour of the last 4% CTax increase. I suggested to Iain that he take it up with you as group leader, which he did, cc'ing me into the email exchange.

I must say Philip, that I found your email replies to the member vague and quite possibly deliberately evasive and as you are clearly an intelligent man that seemed to me to be an attempt at obfuscation.

But I noted that the member seemed to have let the matter rest and I was surprised when he raised it again at Wednesday's meeting.

I agree that the Executive needs to be a friendly and productive forum but that also relies upon the ability of members to trust the information disclosed in those meetings. I'm sorry if you felt the atmosphere was hostile, it's certainly not the way I try to run meetings.

Maybe I'm an idiot and unsuited to politics but actually Philip, I do always TRY at least, to behave in a fair and honourable manner. It's just the way I am and my own sense of morality is more important to me than most other things.

I also always try to do what is best for STCA, which whilst offering little but hassle for me at the moment, I do actually care about.

I hope this (albeit long-winded account) satisfies any concerns you may have had.

Please let me know if you wish to clarify the voting issue for the executive or if you wish me to do so.

Best regards

Lee"

Philip Thomson was also clearly motivated in leading the defection of local Conservative councillors by a foolish and cack handed attempt to unseat him by another Tory councillor, which had the encouragement and assistance of Simon Clarke MP. Another black mark against Simon's poor judgement, among many. It was alleged that this included Simon's constituency office manager Steve Turner contacting other Tory councillors to encourage them to unseat Philip. I don't know if that is true but it certainly fits with Steve Turner's clear dislike for Thomson: I once asked Steve if he would be attending a talk to prospective councillors to be given by Philip. "I'm not going to sit through all that shit," was his colourful reply.

Philip complained about this alleged plot in the letter he sent to the Regional Chairman detailing the faction's planned defection and stating that a Conservative councillor who had previously resigned had done so having failed to unseat him as group leader despite being promised this by the 'parliamentary office'.

He also raised my private comments to him, and him only, hoping that he would have the best interests of the party in mind in deciding how long he would remain group leader. This was unconnected to Simon's activities but arose from clear divisions in the group, Philip regularly turning up and lambasting fellow Tory councillors at Executive Council meetings, and my judgement that Philip was simply not up to the job of leading the Conservative group to future gains, being as tedious as Steve Turner's above comment suggests.

The other complaints in the letter amounted to taking umbrage that the Association now expected its local councillors to keep their word and pay the campaign levy, as all agreed to do so in order to be selected, actually do some work as councillors, and avoid embarrassing the party with controversial, and/or illegal, social media posts, of which I had to deal with many as Chairman. They objected to an injection of integrity and professionalism, in other words.

Cllr Cliff Foggo joined the breakaway, in part at least, motivated by the fact that he had lost out to me in two elections to the association leadership (god knows why missing out on this poison chalice caused him upset!) I had beaten Cliff in a vote of members to become Deputy Chairman Political in 2019 and then Chairman the following year in a lockdown vote on Teams about which he, clearly, was not a happy bunny.

Cliff complained that the vote (which was run over Teams by regional party staff from outside the association and which I had no role in other than as a candidate) had excluded some of his supporters who didn't join the meeting in time, or hadn't pre-registered, or maybe simply hadn't read the email instructions on what to do. They were new fangled procedures and I know that I also had some supporters likewise excluded, but as the vote was run at arms length it was undoubtedly fair. Any glitches were a result of cockup rather than conspiracy, which is more often the case in the Conservative Party.

Cliff had expressed his frustrations during the vote, everyone's mikes being muted by the organisers, by holding his arms up in a X shape on camera like some kind of elderly Power Ranger. This was ignored by the organisers, caused some amusement among the members attending and clearly didn't improve Cliff's mood.

Cliff subsequently complained to CCHQ about the vote in his capacity as 'Membership Secretary' of STCA (a non-existent position under party rules) without first informing the Executive and without declaring himself as a candidate in the disputed vote, which as a Magistrate he should have known better than to do. It annoyed me no end and in a private telephone call with Cliff I must confess to using the F word once, which was not very professional, but as a former military man I'm sure Cliff had heard much worse.

In fairness to Cliff (as I do try to be fair to all concerned), he had done a considerable amount of work for the association on an apparent promise by the former Chairman that he would be a shoo-in for the Chairmanship next time around. His failure to get this promised reward undoubtedly coloured his thoughts on the planned defection.

When I had heard that Philip Thomson and Vera Rider were agitating for a breakaway from the party, I tried to ring Cliff several times, but he did not answer, which is a shame as he would have been a natural replacement 'group leader' (RAF background!) had he stayed in the party and not flounced out with Vera and Phil.

I had more success in persuading the Holmes brothers (no relation) to stay with the party.

Councillors Lee Holmes (again, not me, though the shared name has caused considerable confusion and embarrassment down the years) and Craig Holmes had been elected as Conservative councillors for Skelton West ward in 2019. This had long been a staunchly Labour ward and their election caused much consternation among local Labour activists. Lee and Craig were not typical councillor material, let alone Conservative councillor material, and clearly Philip Thomson, as Conservative group leader, struggled to deal with them. It was clearly a culture clash and generational clash between the rather haughty 'Duchess of Saltburn' as I came to (privately) nickname Thomson, and the rough-around-the-edges Holmes brothers from wild West Skelton.

Thomson would turn up at STCA Executive Council meetings to lambast the Holmes brothers, declaring them unmanageable and 'unfit to be councillors'. I took the view that it was the group leader's job to work with the councillors they had, and that part of the problem at least was Thomson's lack of man-management and communication skills. Hence my *private* suggestion to Philip that he might consider the best interests of the group in deciding how long to remain as leader, which sadly in rather paranoid fashion he took to be another part of the wicked brexiteer plots to unseat him.

Despite Thomson's regular slagging off of the Holmes brothers he was clearly keen to soft-soap them into joining his little rebellion, in order to inflict the maximum damage on me, STCA, Simon Clarke, the party and our candidates (not least Steve Turner) at the upcoming elections in May 2021. I found such behaviour and such duplicity disgusting, then and now, and dropped the Holmes brothers a few messages to inform them of just how much Thomson despised them and that if they were minded to join him in flouncing out they'd better watch their backs. The messages, and a fair amount of work by Simon Clarke in persuading them to stay, worked and Thomson, Rider et al were denied a clean sweep of defections.

Sadly their dishonourable behaviour did cause another very hardworking and good Conservative councillor, Caroline Jackson, to decide to step down, such was the poisonous infighting sparked by Thomson, Jeffery, and Rider in particular. Her loss to the council and to the Conservative group was a great regret.

In a press release in response to Thomson and co's besmirching of the rest of the South Tees Executive, and me as Chairman, the Conservative Party rebutted none of their false accusations and instead thanked them for their previous hard work for the party. In doing so they left their own volunteers hanging. The usual mistreatment of those who keep the whole show on the road. We did, however, have the satisfaction of seeing ALL our local candidates elected at the May elections, despite the rebels actions.

The fracture of relations at South Tees, and the resulting breakaway of some councillors, was perhaps the natural conclusion of the rift that Brexit had caused in the local party, just as it had in the party nationally. Long-standing, traditionalist Tories, of a certain post-war generation, who viewed the EU as some kind of bulwark against future conflict in Europe, looked upon Brexit as a dangerous fracture of familial relations across the continent. Those with a background in commerce and trade, the traditional Conservative pro-business bedrock, also viewed the disruption caused by brexit as a wholly regrettable and negative consequence of the Little Englander attitudes of the newer Ukipper influx to the party.

Two personalities personified these differences locally. Our association President Iain Alexander, a businessman whose entire business was dependent upon trade across the EU, and who came from that generation who looked back upon wartime divisions in Europe with such apprehension. Somebody with actual, real-world experience of international commerce and the benefits of barrier free trade across the continent.

The other was Simon Clarke MP, sometime cabinet minister under the Johnson and Truss (mal)administrations. Sadly, whether through inexperience (he was only, and unexpectedly, elected in the otherwise grim Tory general election of 2017), true-believer zealotry, or malice, Simon only made those divisions in the local party worse. Indeed he seemed to take pleasure in antagonising those he saw as 'wets'. The fact this phrase, so beloved of 1980s Thatcherites, was a regular part of Simon's vocabulary speaks volumes about his own right-wing Conservative instincts and tendency to view others of differing opinions in the party as being outsiders, or unworthy of the name 'Conservative.'

Whatever the causes of Simon's antagonistic attitudes, it was a foolish way to behave for any MP, let alone one newly elected and without much experience either inside or outside of politics. It also made for festering hostilities in a local party with an already long history of feuds and falling-outs.

For the record, I say all this as a Leave voter, and a life long eurosceptic, though one who was surprised to have been on the winning side in the 2016 referendum. For a 'wet' I am not, and I view *most* of what Margaret Thatcher set out to achieve in the 1980s as both necessary and successful.

But crucially, I was the type of Conservative who believes that any political party, including the Tories, *must* be a broad church if it is to thrive. Picking fights over narrow doctrinal differences or swinging to political extremes of unelectable purity is a disease usually suffered by the Labour Party, and it had kept them out of power for most of the post-war period. Sadly, it seems to be an infection picked up by an increasingly right-wing and intolerant Conservative Party. How far and for how long the Tories traipse down what might be described as the 'Corbynista' trail will likely determine how long they are out of power for.

As Chairman of South Tees I viewed my role as trying to hold the local party together and to make all shades of centre-right opinion feel welcome, including those who voted Remain and even those who were at heart strongly committed to the UK in europe. My experience with losing half a dozen councillors to defections might make this statement seem hard to believe. However, my falling out with those in that group was certainly not doctrinal or even over differences of policy. It was far more a difference of principles, in that I believed that councillors should tell the truth, honour commitments given and play as part of a team. In that sense my failings were more those of naivety than doctrinal purity.

I tried very hard to persuade Iain Alexander to continue as our association President, especially once I got wind that he was minded to stand down. Word was that he was waiting to see how Boris Johnson's 'oven ready' Brexit deal would affect his own business of trading chemicals across the UK and Europe, before making a decision, though he was plainly not enamoured of Brexit or the general direction of travel the party was taking under Johnson.

In a telephone call I urged him to stay on and made plain my own view that the Conservative Party must remain a broad church and that views such as his would be welcome, certainly on my watch as Chairman.

However, my entreaties failed and he stepped down and took the usually steady flow of donations to association funds that normally come with a well connected and wealthy President. A broad church also garners broad donations.

I understand that the ill-feeling between Simon Clarke and Alexander was such that at association dinners Simon had tried to alter the seating plan in order to avoid being seated near the association president and had been caught out doing so. Such behaviour is just juvenile, ill befitting an MP and shows that distinct lack of judgement that has become such a feature of Clarke's career. His last ditch backing of Johnson even after the Chris Pincher debacle, then backing the wholly unsuitable Truss for PM, then back to backing Johnson's abortive bid to return as Tory leader has seen Clarke's ministerial career flounder and deservedly so. In fairness (and as you know, I alway *try* to be fair) Clarke's an intelligent guy, but his judgement, on a whole range of issues, is abysmal.

It may well be that such a lack of judgement is now the norm in the Conservative Party, and that splits and personal vendettas of the kind I endured at South Tees are now also the norm nationally. The manoeuvring and intriguing surrounding challenges to Sunak's leadership (not least by the newly enobled Sir Simon) suggest the party is now almost ungovernable under any leader. If so, that mirrors my own experience of trying to keep the factions together at South Tees, and augurs disastrously for the party's future.

Chapter 15 - General Mayhem

General Mayhem was a wonderful old duffer and South Tees Conservatives' longest serving member. When not regaling us with tales of his derring-do during the First Boer War he was still, despite his advanced age of 112, a regular leaflet deliverer and canvasser on our campaign sessions, and as such a great stalwart of the Conservative Party. In many ways very typical of its current membership.

Admittedly his slow gait, on two walking sticks, meant that in a two hour session before our usual trip to the pub he may only have managed to deliver a couple of leaflets. Occasionally, he also had to be dragged away from voters when haranguing them about the danger posed by 'the Boche', but nonetheless his enthusiastic support of the Tory party really was quite a thing to witness.

I jest, of course.

Though, thinking back, some of the characters I encountered in my time in the Conservative Party were no less eye-catching, or for that matter jaw-dropping, than the entirely fictional good General mentioned above (the only part of this sorry tale I have made up, I hasten to add).

The 'general mayhem' I do want to address in this chapter are some of the many, *slightly* less serious matters I had to deal with as Chairman, to clear up the mess often left in their wake by Tory activists and councillors. Some of these lesser events nonetheless involved law breaking and would have caused considerable embarrassment to the party without my diplomatic skills (which despite appearances to the contrary in this book, do actually exist.)

The events detailed give an indication of the nature of the current Conservative Party and its elected officials and members. They don't paint the most attractive of pen portraits but are typical of some of the behaviours within the party at South Tees, and no doubt elsewhere. In the party's defence (there's that bloody fair-mindedness again) I would expect that other parties also have their fair share of rogue members and misbehaviour.

Political parties are by their nature, and quite rightly, a microcosm of society as a whole, which from my experience also contains its fair share of eccentrics, the slightly unhinged, and downright mad.

Or it may be that politics attracts the wrong people. Precisely the wrong people, who would be the very last wrong people you would want, in an ideal world, to be placed in charge of running a bath, let alone a country of very nearly 70 million people.

If that is a depressing conclusion to come to, then I'm afraid to say it is a conclusion one could reasonably come to from reading this book. It is a conclusion I have certainly come to from my experiences within the Conservative Party. And I must, out of fairness, include myself among the 'wrong people' group. For *I* was also attracted to politics.

Alternatively, you may take the more charitable view that politics attracts a broad cross section of society and as such it is bound to include a fair number of 'wrong 'uns'.

The following tales are about a selection of those 'wrong 'uns'.

The others I will hold back for a sequel. Enjoy.

Section 106

Although the General Mayhem character noted above is entirely fictional he does share some of the traits of the other *ahem* 'characters' I had to deal with in my time at South Tees. One couple in particular, though hard-working and dedicated activists within the party, were widely regarded as walking unexploded bombs when allowed out on the campaign trail.

One of them also delighted in causing havoc and pursuing vendettas in their role as a local association officer, yet had somehow become a candidate in a rather fraught contest in the local elections. All of this meant that South Tees Conservatives was about to become embroiled in yet another police investigation that threatened to blacken the name of the party, at a crucial time when a general election could have been just around the corner.

As is often the case in politics the origins of this sorry tale can be found in an unhappy parting of the ways, in this example that being among Conservative councillors in the association.

For my predecessor as Chairman, Malcolm Griffiths, had himself suffered a breakaway of councillors prior to the later defections we suffered under my chairmanship (see the chapter 'Councillors are Revolting'.)

The origins of this split were personality clashes: the defectors couldn't stand Malcolm and I believe the feeling was mutual.

It may also have been that the councillors concerned had sniffed the air and had a sense of the direction the political wind was blowing. Which by early 2019 under Theresa May's premiership was distinctly against the Tory party and in favour of independents. They may have calculated, quite rightly, that they stood a better chance of re-election by dumping an unpopular party badge.

The strange rivalries and territorialism that exists when former associations are merged into the kind of federation that South Tees had become, also undoubtedly played a role in this sad political divorce.

Three constituencies and their relevant associations had some time before been merged to become the 'South Tees Federation', headquartered in Guisborough in the one marginal constituency we covered and, in fairness, in quite a central location for the federation area as a whole. However, it's also fair to say the members of the former Middlesbrough association, which had instead become a mere branch of STCA, were not keen on this arrangement of what they regarded as 'rule from Guisborough'.

When some of those councillors came up for re-selection under party rules prior to the 2019 local elections, they refused to travel the six or seven miles to the federation office in Guisborough for their re-selection meetings and instead opted to stand again in their wards as independents. This meant the party had lost the majority of its councillors in Middlesbrough, of whom there weren't many to begin with.

Now it might be that if the federation management had agreed to travel to Middlesbrough to hold the meetings then these defections may not have happened. This is before my time on the executive of STCA but it seemed that neither side was willing to move to meet the other, both literally and metaphorically. Maybe some kind of Cold War summit could have been held on the demarcation line, a la North and South Korea, between the two former association areas, but this seems not to have been considered either.

Re-selection of serving councillors, whilst required by party rules, should normally be a formality in my opinion, unless there are genuine and serious concerns about the sitting councillor's commitment, work-rate, capacity or unacceptable and publicly stated views.

No such concerns were present in these cases as far as I am aware and their reselections should have been waved through with minimum fuss. For not to do so, when you have popular and seemingly hard-working Tory councillors, now aggrieved and standing as independents, in some of the few winnable wards you have, only opens up a whole world of pain. As we were about to find out.

Inexplicably, the association Executive, our Campaign Manager and Simon Clarke, the sitting MP for the constituency in which the rebel wards were situated, seem to have decided to compound this mess by fighting a full campaign against the rebels, throwing a whole load of money, materials and activist's time into what looked like a wholly unwinnable fight from the outset. In a move that was really stunningly, jaw-droppingly, incomprehensibly stupid they also chose perhaps the least suitable candidates to front this fight: the hardworking, but feisty and unpredictable elderly couple mentioned above.

The pain in this unwinnable war of our own making was about to go legal and drag in both Middlesbrough Council and Cleveland Police.

For it was alleged by a voter in the ward that one of our candidates had rocked up on their doorstep and made a variety of unflattering and unproven allegations about the sitting former Tory councillors. The allegations touched on concerns about the use of funds raised by the former Middlesbrough branch quiz night and also alleged that the former Tory councillors had been 'thrown out of the party'.

Unfortunately for our candidate the said voter was a friend of the rebel councillors and reported straight back to them on what had allegedly been said, and they in turn high-tailed it to the Elections Officer at the council to make a complaint. Who in turn called in Cleveland Police.

For making unproven allegations against opponents in elections is not only poor politics (it's overly negative and makes you look rather bitter) it can also contravene Section 106 of the Representation of the People Act 1983, leading to distressing police investigations and possible prosecution. The investigation began almost immediately and would run and run.

I'm not going to touch on the allegations other than to say that IF the quiz funds had belonged to the branch, and IF they had been disposed of without the consent of the federation executive, then technically this would be against Conservative Party rules. For under those rules property of any branch is strictly the property of the whole federation, not the branch alone. I say 'IF' because record keeping at South Tees was as bad as the relationships between its leading members, which was very bad indeed, and it's not clear what decisions were ever taken regarding the funds, or by who.

Technically, the rebel councillors *were* in the process of being expelled and barred from the party, as standing against party candidates in an election leads to a mandatory expulsion for a period of years. However, it may have been stretching it to say that they *had been* 'thrown out of the party', especially if this was being linked to the issue about quiz night funds.

Regardless, it was very foolish to be raising any of this on the doorstep with voters at all, for the reasons above.

But interestingly, as the police investigation got underway, our candidate denied having said any of these things at all.

Unfortunately for them, when the matter was first raised with the council our Campaign Manager had been made aware of the allegations. When he contacted the candidate by email to warn against any such negative campaigning, the candidate had effectively confirmed they *had merely* raised the issue of the quiz funds and simply wanted answers.

When these emails were turned over to Cleveland Police at their request by our Campaign Manager, our candidate had a new target in their vendetta: our Campaign Manager for 'stabbing them in the back'

The candidate concerned was also elected to the STCA Executive Council as an officer of the association in April 2019 at the same elections where I had been elected Deputy Chairman Political. As such we were thrown together as the modernising faction on a federation still under the chairmanship of Malcolm Griffiths. It's fair to say that Malcolm and the candidate didn't get on, references to Malcolm as 'the poison dwarf' and a 'little shit' were certainly uttered at executive meetings, if not read into the minutes. This ill-will was made worse once the police investigation got underway as the candidate felt Malcolm was not supporting them in contesting the allegations, or in providing evidence that might clear them.

For all I was often exasperated by the glacial state of progress under Malcolm's chairmanship and his occasionally boorish manner, and had a number of fallings out with him, we actually got on reasonably well and I was never impressed by the abuse that came at him from some of his opponents in the association. Especially when that abuse and infighting looked like going public, as it occasionally did.

The candidate, being on the same modernising and, as they saw it, 'anti-Malcolm' wing of the executive would occasionally say something outrageously untrue, demonstrably so, about Malcom's leadership or actions in executive meetings, and tip me a theatrical wink whilst doing so. All very pantomime but not very edifying.

And so the allegations of misbehaviour on the campaign trail had a certain credence when they came up, even before being apparently confirmed by the emails requested by police.

Even so, the police investigation, into an individual in their seventies (even the modernisers are old in the Tory party) and in poor health, seemed a somewhat excessive use of police powers. This was all the more so as the complainants in the case had already instructed solicitors and were threatening a defamation action, and so could have dealt with the matter through the civil courts if they had wanted to.

When election day came and went and the complainants (predictably) won by a landslide, absolutely thrashing their Conservative opponents, the need for a police investigation and action against our candidate became all the more questionable. Yet it rumbled on with a requirement for interviews under caution, causing immense stress to a couple in poor health anyway.

At this point, and no support for the accused being forthcoming from the association or party, I decided to do whatever I could to try to end the stress of the investigation in my capacity as Deputy Chairman, but making clear I wasn't acting on behalf of the Conservative Party or South Tees association.

I emailed the investigating officer, his direct superior, and the Chief Constable of Cleveland Police, questioning whether continuing with this investigation was either in the public interest, given the frailty of the accused and the actual election result, and also questioning whether it was an effective use of police time and resources.

Cleveland Police was afterall one of the worst performing forces in the country at that time.

I also threw in a slew of Conservative Party rules about use of funds and asked if the investigation had the time to look into what had actually been agreed in the past within the branch or federation, and pointing out just how resource intensive that would be, but that it would be required to actually rule out a possible defence of 'reasonable belief'.

I even threw in an email to the Director of Public Prosecutions whose agreement is necessary before any prosecutions can be brought under S106 anyway, noting the rarity of any such prosecutions, and that none had ever been brought against a *losing* candidate in the past.

In fairness to the investigating officer, who contacted me by phone to discuss the case at length, he was a thoroughly reasonable guy and was merely doing his job and did actually sympathise with the accused for the mess they had gotten themselves into. Sympathy that wasn't natural, given the histrionics he often received from the accused in return for merely conducting his investigation.

After several weeks more, and much more stress and histrionics, the investigation was quietly concluded with no further action being taken. A sensible and just conclusion.

I doubt very much whether my intervention made a blind bit of difference, being a very small fish indeed, but to the accused I was now their 'hero' and a bottle of Jack Daniels was offered, and gratefully received, by way of thanks.

I urged them to put it all behind them but to learn from it, and not to do anything to risk antagonising their victorious opponents, who still had a civil action open to them. I also warned them not to hold events against our Campaign Manager, who had clearly had no choice but to cooperate with the police investigation by handing over the emails.

Unfortunately, that advice went largely unheeded and I was soon to be transformed from their 'hero' into their arch enemy.

"Boris, Boris, Boris!"

The calling of the snap Brexit election in winter 2019, and the suspension by the party of Malcolm as Chairman over his ill-judged comments on Facebook, saw this accidental Deputy Chairman thrust into being an accidental Chairman of South Tees during an utterly crucial general election.

As the only deputy Chairman elected at the last AGM, my fellow Deputy being an unelected shoo-in for the less glamorous 'Deputy Chairman Membership' position, I felt I had the more legitimate claim to step up as acting Chairman, and my colleagues agreed.

My fellow association officer, the troublesome candidate above, expected me to call an immediate executive council meeting, no doubt hoping to settle some scores with Malcolm's supporters on the executive, but with an election in full swing, that wasn't my priority. Winning it was.

We were fortunate at South Tees to still have our full time Campaign Manager, who was well-organised, if not well-liked by some. My first concern was ensuring that they had the resources to throw into retaining Middlesbrough South and East Cleveland for the party, the contests in Redcar and Middlesbrough being regarded (wrongly in the case of Redcar) as almost certain Labour wins.

For most of the rest of the campaign things went very smoothly, with lots of campaign sessions being held almost every day, mostly generating a very positive vibe and feedback, and turning up at many myself as an active, hands-on (boots on) Chairman.

However, that smooth campaign was about to come to a juddering halt and our erstwhile candidates from the ugly fight at the May local elections were the, not unpredictable, cause.

In the largely council estate ward of Hemlington, on the southern edge of Middlesbrough, our 'heroes' had been canvassing with Simon Clarke, though fortunately or unfortunately, depending which way you look at it, out of sight and earshot of the MP himself.

Knocking on the door of a supposedly sympathetic target voter (the computer algorithms used by the party to identify potential supporters were proving pretty ropey at that time) they had received a less than welcoming response from the resident. It was later alleged by them that something along the lines of 'fudge the Tories' had been said and an argument ensued.

The next day, Steve Turner took a call from the resident complaining about the Tory canvassers behaviour, alleging that a 5 to 10 minute argument had ensued when she said she didn't like the Tories and wouldn't be voting for them, with the canvassers behaviour being both aggressive and at times childish. In response to an expression of opposition to the 'Bedroom Tax' the resident alleged that one of the canvassers had replied that they didn't know anything about benefits as they had 'worked all their life.' Taken, not unreasonably, to be a dig at them and benefit claimants generally.

The resident further alleged that a neighbour had felt it necessary to step between them and one of the canvassers who was aggressively jabbing their finger at the resident. Eventually the unpleasant and unseemly argument ended with the canvassers moving off down the street allegedly chanting "Boris! Boris! Boris!"

The allegations seemed to have credibility, given what others of us had witnessed from the two in the past, and a decision was taken that day between Turner, Clarke and our Campaign Manager to stand those canvassers down from campaigning for the rest of the election campaign. Turner called on the pair that day to hear their side of events but to let them know that they couldn't continue campaigning until further notice. As big Boris fans (clearly) and really very dedicated, if volatile, Tory campaigners this no doubt came as a big shock and disappointment.

In my guide to canvassing for local activists, reproduced later in this chapter, I make the point very clearly that as party volunteers we are not there to get into debates, let alone arguments or, god forbid, fights with voters. It's not only a very bad look, it's an almighty waste of precious time.

My advice was always that if you sense hostility to the Conservative cause, politely make your excuses and leave. Depressingly, in these increasingly aggressive times, for reasons of personal safety as well, simply move on.

There is no point wasting any time at all trying to persuade a voter who will never vote Tory in a million years. Move on and spend your valuable time on those who may be persuaded by our message, or those who are already convinced, but who need a reminder or chivvying to actually get out and vote.

When I was told as Chairman later that day what had happened I agreed wholeheartedly with the decision to remove them from campaigning. Clearly my advice at the end of the police investigation to take care when talking to voters and to avoid negative campaigning hadn't been heeded in any way, shape or form.

I spoke to one of the suspended canvassers later that day, and although they denied large chunks of the allegations made against them, their recollection that the resident was still in a dressing gown at lunchtime tended to confirm, in my mind at least, that their alleged comments on benefits and working all their life were undoubtedly true.

Yet again I advised them to take it easy, enjoy the break from campaigning, avoid negativity or retribution, and learn from the experience.

As it turns out, such an aspiration only showed my usual naivety.

For just a few days later the couple and their aggressive behaviour reared their ugly heads again.

Following the stunning landslide victory on December 12th the party faithful, or those in the know at least, got wind of a celebratory visit to the North East by the all-conquering Boris Johnson. The venue, to rub Labour's nose in the Tory decimation of their former Red Wall strongholds, would be Tony Blair's old constituency of Sedgefield.

And so we travelled in some numbers to Sedgefield Cricket Club to welcome the 'great man' himself and hear his usual ebullient bluster and self-congratulatory boosterism (this time arguably well deserved.) When I arrived I spied a couple of friends from South Tees and took up position with a good view of the likely speech platform in what was a crowded and slightly chaotic clubhouse.

After a while we ourselves were spied by the canvassing couple who had caused such consternation before polling day. They joined us and almost immediately launched into a diatribe against Steve Turner, for 'stabbing them in their backs' by removing them from campaigning and believing a load of 'Labour lies' about them.

It was embarrassing to say the least, that a celebratory occasion was being marred by angry raised voices and yet more negativity and vendetta-fighting. I calmly tried to change the subject without much success and before long one of the canvassers was deploying their customary jabbing finger against one of our local councillors, wholly blameless in the events they were clearly still very angry about. Thankfully Boris arrived and provided a distraction that even our angry canvassers couldn't ignore.

It was yet another example however of this couple's capacity for causing chaos and ill-will wherever they went. A capacity that early in the new year, with a local by-election in the offing, couldn't be ignored any longer, for such was the fear of what further havoc they might wreak on the campaign trail that the decision was taken to formally intervene in their behaviour.

Forgery

Towards the end of my time as South Tees Chairman I received a phone call from a colleague within the association who also happened to be a local councillor. At the time, which was late afternoon, I was laid flat out on the floor glossing skirting boards with white gloss paint. This detail is relevant as I'm not sure whether it was the paint fumes, or exasperation at yet another South Tees scandal, that prompted my slightly hysterical response. Hysterical as in laughter.

My colleague informed me that they had been caught out forging a signature on official nomination papers for a local council contest in which they were acting as the candidate's agent. It wasn't a case of forging nominees signatures, which would have been a more serious matter, but rather the candidate's signature on the 'Consent to Nomination' form which the candidate had mistakenly failed to sign before heading away for the weekend on holiday. Unhelpfully, this was just before the submission deadline for the forms.

In a 'moment of madness' and to avoid the nomination being invalidated, my colleague had copied the candidate's signature from one of the other endless forms he *had* signed onto the consent form. Mimicking the signature in an act I later charitably termed as 'transcribing' when explaining the matter to other officers in the association. The candidate *had* consented to being our candidate so the act of forging his signature wasn't entirely dishonest, but nonetheless it did amount to forging official documents in an election.

All this would have gone unnoticed (the clerk to the council had accepted the forms when submitted by the agent as valid, and as such the candidate was validly nominated) were it not for the fact the candidate, on returning from his weekend away, had discovered his unsigned consent form at home, signed it, and taken it into the council. The fact that the candidate was a former policeman, and took matters of forgery very seriously, obviously didn't help matters.

As I lay on my back on a hard laminate wood floor, paint pot to one side and engulfed in paint fumes I couldn't help but chuckle as the story unfolded. It *was* a serious matter but quite frankly after two years or so of dealing with this kind of stuff at South Tees I was losing the will to live, or actually handle yet another case in the constant stream of cock-ups and misbehaviour. Or I was high on paint fumes.

I was also naturally sympathetic to my colleague who was fundamentally a decent human being and a good, hard-working councillor, and who had been very supportive of me as Chairman and in helping to deal with the umpteen other scandals we'd had recently.

A case of gamekeeper turned poacher perhaps?

OK, I said, what's done is done, and you've held your hands up to the council, who had informed police of the matter, you're just going to have to be contrite and take your raps as they come. It wasn't the end of the world, I laughed, both trying to lighten the mood with an element of pastoral concern for my colleague who was clearly bereft at what they had done, and quite possibly under the paint's influence. We ended the call shortly thereafter.

Taking a break from the painting, the seriousness of the matter began to sink in and I called my colleague back and said you'd better phone Simon Clarke's office and give them a heads-up on what's happened lest the scandal becomes public knowledge. I could have done it but to be frank I was sick of pulling other people's chestnuts out of the fire, so to speak. I also said I would have to inform the 'professional' party staff locally about what had happened.

Later I took a call from Simon Clarke's office manager to say they had been contacted by the candidate. They were furious at the prospect of being elected under a fraudulent nomination, were demanding to speak to Simon Clarke (who was no doubt busy with ministerial affairs) and threatening to go to the press or, even worse, our LibDem opponents in the contest, and could I speak to him?

At this stage the whole thing threatened to engulf our MP as well, who rather like the aircraft carrier in a naval group, must be protected from attack at all costs. Yes, I would happily speak to the candidate who was also one of our local members, but who I didn't know personally.

And he was irate. But with justifiable reason to be so, as if he was elected the whole affair would undoubtedly go public and his good name would be tarnished as corrupt, given the actions of his agent. Over a good twenty minutes I attempted to calm him and talk him down.

By all means, I said, go to the police although I assured him they had already been informed and were looking into the matter, but I questioned why a Conservative would want to go running to our opponents the LibDems to tell them all? The LibDems are notoriously one of the dirtiest parties when it comes to local and national campaigning. Desperation in being the much maligned third party often breeding the use of some pretty underhand and dishonest campaign tactics on their behalf.

I assured our candidate, quite bizarrely I suppose, that I would do all I could to have their nomination declared invalid by the local council or the Electoral Commission and their name removed from the ballot paper, so that there would be no danger whatsoever of them being elected on a false prospectus. If this failed I would ensure, as Chairman, that not a single penny of association money, or time or energy, would be expended on trying to get them elected. Not a thing, nada, zilch. We would do absolutely f#*k all to aid their election. All in all an odd promise to make to a party candidate.

But this promise of doing absolutely nothing to help their election seemed to work, the candidate was suitably pacified, and was content to let the police investigate the matter and for me to attempt to have his nomination overturned. More work for muggins here.

I contacted the local borough council to see what we could do to overturn the nomination and spoke to their legal bods, who were extremely helpful. They also happened to be of the same mind as me, that allowing the nomination to stand and the election to go ahead would both look ridiculous, given we all now knew the nomination was invalid, and risked wasting public money on an election that would have to be re-run if our candidate won.

However, they had already contacted the Electoral Commission to make all these same points to them but they were adamant that as the council clerk had checked and had accepted the nomination papers as valid upon submission, the later uncovery of forgery could not invalidate that initial acceptance. This seems a ludicrous stance to take but the council legal officers said the Electoral Commissions view seemed entrenched. They were seeking legal counsel's opinion on the matter to try to persuade the Commission otherwise, but I was more than welcome to contact the Commission as well to argue the toss.

This I did, and in a long telephone conversation with their specialist on this area of electoral law I couldn't budge them either, not even with all my frustrated-lawyer, law-graduate, national-courtroom-advocacy-champion powers of persuasion. Neither deploying the 'mischief rule' nor urging them to look at parliament's intention in drafting the legislation (which plainly couldn't have been that uncovered forgery should be overlooked) would have them budge from their position that the nomination papers, once deemed valid, cannot be invalidated.

Which in purely technical legal terms is 'bullshit', in my humble opinion!

But the Commission was not for turning and we were stuck with an election costing several thousand pounds of taxpayers money that might well have to be re-run if the wrong candidate (ie. ours) won.

So we did absolutely nothing to promote that candidate nor encourage voters to vote Conservative and luckily for us, and my colleague who would probably have been forced to cover the costs of a re-run election, we lost. And having won by a kind of default in a non-contest our opponent, who likely knew about the whole mess, wasn't inclined to raise the matter publicly either. Lest it diminish their victory!

The 'professional' party, once informed of the forgery, insisted that the association suspend the member concerned, which isn't strictly how the rules are supposed to work. As CCHQ also has the power to suspend any member anyway, this seemed like yet another example of the centre dumping more work on the poor beleaguered volunteers on the ground (ie. me) So I contacted all our local Executive Council members to detail the whole debacle and recommend suspension whilst the matter was resolved. So to insulate the party, and our local elected politicians from any resulting damage should the affair go public. This was agreed, reluctantly, as people were sympathetic with the 'author' of the mess. As was I.

So, yet another narrow scrape for South Tees Conservatives, though the police investigation was still to run its course, and here things get a little murky. For that investigation apparently concluded that no actual laws had been broken in forging a signature on official nomination papers, which does seem a little odd to say the least.

My colleague was active in the Freemasons, and whilst I'm not for a moment (I've offended enough powerful people with this book as it stands!) suggesting there were any 'favours' done by other potential Freemasons in Cleveland Police, I'll let the more conspiratorially minded among you mull that one over.

The only consequence for this electoral fraud was that the local council carried out disciplinary proceedings against the member concerned, on the quiet, which seemed to amount to apologising and copying out a thousand lines of 'I must not commit forgery.'

This might not be strictly true, but it is an amusing thought.

Theft

It has become something of a tradition in leafleting, among some activists, to steal opponents leaflets from letterboxes if you come across them whilst delivering your own. In fairness to the Conservative Party, this apparently applies to all parties, given news reports featuring a LibDem candidate caught on security cameras swiping leaflets a few years ago.

I've never done this, both on the basis that it's probably technically theft, and also on the rather romantic notion that if politics is a battle of ideas, you should at least let voters read your opponent's ideas before hopefully judging them to be dreadful. Not swipe them from their letterboxes before they've even seen them. Clearly I'm a fool to myself in this, as in so much else.

I *would* judge it acceptable to read an opponent's leaflets and even take a photo of it to see what rubbish they are saying, especially if it's about you, but then place the leaflet back in the letterbox for the intended voter.

However, I have occasionally seen leaflets 'lifted' by others and occasionally tutted disapprovingly at it. In writing a campaign guide for local activists (reproduced below for your amusement) while Deputy Chairman Political, on avoiding the perils of leafleting (vicious dogs, slippery steps etc) I also made the point that swiping opponents leaflets is not acceptable and probably breaks the law.

On one occasion, whilst leafleting with quite a senior figure I witnessed them do just this and jokingly commented to them that they "really should know better"

And given their background and position, they really should have known better.

(I'm not naming the individual as in any libel action it would really be a case of my word against theirs, and that's not a good enough legal defence. Though I know what I saw, and it may not be the only fraudulent behaviour they engaged in.)

STCA CAMPAIGNING ADVICE FOR CANDIDATES AND VOLUNTEERS

- Wear smart, or smart-casual, but comfortable clothing and shoes. Comfort is king when leafleting.

- Check the weather forecast (most leaflets don't like rain)

- **Watch your footing when approaching front doors: hidden steps and sprained ankles won't help your campaign! Resin driveways can be slippery when wet.**

- Use your judgement about whether to cross lawns etc between neighbouring properties. Trampling someone's prize begonias won't win you many votes!

- Look for the letterbox on your approach. There is nothing worse than trudging up a long driveway to find the letterbox was at the gate!

- Consider using a glove (leaving one hand bare to manipulate leaflets) a stick or spatula when posting leaflets through (letterboxes can be sharp and unforgiving) Satchels help with carrying leaflets

- Try to work out the optimum route between properties. Avoid criss-crossing roads unnecessarily. Use your time as efficiently as possible.

- It has been known for leafletters to remove opposition leaflets they come across, though strictly this is theft and best avoided! Maybe take a photo to know what the opposition are saying and feed back to STCA.

- **Avoid aggressive dogs: no leaflet is worth a bite, stitches and a tetanus jab. Beware dogs (and occasional cats) that lurk behind letterboxes waiting to snap at fingers.**

- Leave garden gates as you found them (ie. close them behind you if closed when you arrived). If dogs or children are likely to be present close gates behind you when approaching the door as well. You don't want to waste time chasing Fido up the street!

- Say hello to children but avoid engaging in conversation. Parents can be naturally wary of strangers. No kissing babies!

- Smile and say hello to local residents, even when just leafleting. Introduce yourself and engage in conversation if you have time. It could be a vote won.

Canvassing

- Personal contact between voters and the candidate is key to winning votes. Use any data we have to target known and possible supporters.

- **Do not get into arguments with people: we are there to persuade voters, not row with them. Friendly debate is acceptable but avoid wasting time on lost causes. If** people are aggressive, say "sorry to bother you" and walk away. Your safety is paramount.

- Beware spending *too much* time with voters who may be opposition supporters waylaying you. Even our supporters may delay you speaking to persuadable voters.

- **Do NOT make false statements about other candidates (or yourself) This may be an offence under S106 RPA 1983 and has led to police investigations in the past.** If in doubt, say nowt! Negative campaigning is best avoided anyway.

- Don't volunteer controversial but irrelevant opinions. A local councillor can do nothing about certain issues but you could lose a potential vote by being too vocal. **Remember your objective is purely to gain votes**. Try to get voters to express their views first and agree with them or keep schtum as appropriate.

- Avoid being seen to agree with offensive (ie. racist etc) opinions. Even sagely nodding your head could make a bad impression. Challenge, change the subject or move on.

- Don't over-promise things you can't possibly deliver. Voters see through this.

- **Don't risk offending hundreds of voters to please just a few by taking up marginal causes. Think politically.**

- Don't be afraid to admit you don't know enough about a particular issue, or the answer to a particular question. Offer to look into it instead. This is far better than winging it and pretending to be an expert when you're not!

- **LISTEN** to local residents: they are likely to be more expert on local issues than you are.

- Search social media (Facebook, Instagram etc) for local community or interest groups to learn about local issues and maybe get in touch.

- Search local media/websites for background information/issues about your ward. Do some research in advance.

- **Most of all enjoy! Campaigning is an adventure.**

Black Lives Matter

Much of my involvement with South Tees Conservatives took place against the backdrop of the covid pandemic and the various lockdowns which were imposed in an attempt to control it. These lockdowns undoubtedly changed the experience of chairing a local association and the way the party functioned. They also probably contributed to some of the madness that ensued during those heady lockdown days, as isolation and cabin fever appeared to afflict some. Possibly myself included.

The revolt by local councillors was undoubtedly affected by the lockdown and wouldn't have occurred in the way it did, if at all, without the restrictions that prevented face to face meetings, and left much to the somewhat blunter tools of email and Zoom.

Likewise, in the heated days of covid restrictions in early summer 2020, when the death of George Floyd at the hands of US police prompted widespread protests in the UK I was called upon to adjudicate whether certain local councillors had overstepped the mark and ventured into racism in some of their comments on social media. The fact one of them had faced previous accusations in the local press of racism due to earlier facebook posts, and that both of them were hate figures for local Labour supporters only made that task more fraught.

One of our councillors, Craig Holmes (no relation) had set up the Skelton in Cleveland facebook page several years before and it had become easily the most popular forum for local news, advertising and feuding in the Skelton area. It had also played a vital role in getting the councillor, and his brother Lee Holmes (not me), elected for the Tories in what had always previously been a staunch Labour ward.

In the fevered days following the appalling death of George Floyd, as covid rule breaking Black Lives Matter protests occurred in London and elsewhere, and far right counter protests sprung up in response, debate about the wrongs and rights spilled over onto facebook, not least in Skelton, a place about as far removed from inner-city London as it's possible to be.

The Holmes brothers were always active on their facebook page, as were their critics in the local community, not least left-wing Momentum activists in the local Labour party. It's fair to say the hatred was mutual, and the temperature over 'black lives matter' rising to boiling point.

Hundreds of posts, reposts, replies and responses were pinging back and forth on the page, all exacerbated by the emotive nature of the issue, and crucially, the magnifying effect of everybody being restrained and cooped up by covid restrictions. Tempers were reaching boiling point as allegations of racism, white privilege and colonialism were thrown about from the left and counter allegations of extremism, hatred of the UK and anti-white prejudice were thrown back in retaliation.

After bubbling along at boiling point for several days I was contacted by our local CCHQ contact and asked to consider whether our councillors had overstepped the mark and were guilty of racism and whether suspension should be considered. Wearily, I said I would take a look.

Firstly, I had to request access to the page as I wasn't a member. Once this was granted I began a long, long trawl of posts and replies made by the Holmes brothers, many of which couldn't be understood or placed in context without reading the often long and involved posts they were replying to. It became a long and exhausting process, made worse by the vitriol spewing from both sides in the debate. If it can be dignified with such a term.

By this stage the exchanges had made their way into the local press, with reports making reference to current allegations of racism from the councillors in the BLM exchanges on facebook, and the previous allegations levelled at posts made years before by Lee Holmes before they became a councillor. In the fevered atmosphere of covid lockdown restrictions AND the BLM furore this seemingly low level stuff on facebook had capacity to become newsworthy nationally, with all the potential damage to the party's reputation that that entailed.

It was clear, in my judgement, that both councillors sailed close to the wind in the posts on facebook, especially in response to some pretty vitriolic attacks from their left wing opponents. Raising the issue of islamist attacks on white victims in the UK, as they did, in response to allegations of systemic racism in policing and society as a whole, wasn't big and it wasn't clever. It allowed their opponents to make allegations of racism and islamophobia in response, which had in turn made their way from social media to the mainstream media. But was it racist?

As a great believer in freedom of speech, but also as someone with a visceral hatred of racism and all other forms of irrational prejudice, this judgement placed me in quite a quandary. The councillors replies to attacks on facebook were combative and challenging, they controversially brought in the issue of islamist extremism in this country, and the violence that has resulted, as some kind of counter argument to the BLM assertion that racism is endemic in white people. It was an inflammatory comparison, certainly to the left wing mob the brothers seemed to attract on facebook, yet it was a comparison there to be made in a society that values freedom of speech.

On the basis that such a comparison was neither intrinsically racist nor islamophobic and that the only restrictions on freedom of speech in a free country should be to prevent the incitement of violence or hatred, I felt that the councillors' comments, though undoubtedly controversial, had not crossed the line into racism, islamophobia or other forbidden conduct.

After hours of trawling through some pretty unedifying posts from both sides in the debate, I felt in need of a good hot shower. When I relayed my conclusion back to CCHQ that the councillors, whilst combative and controversial, had not broken party rules I was asked to take screenshots of the worst examples of their comments. To which I replied I'd already spent hours considering this matter and if they wanted screenshots they should join the group and take them themselves. On the basis I was a volunteer, whereas they're paid to deal with this crap.

In addition to the complaints made to the media over the BLM facebook exchanges a complaint was also made against the councillors to Redcar and Cleveland Council, alleging their comments had breached their Code of Conduct. Some time later, after an investigation, the Council's conduct panel reached the same conclusion I had. Freedom of speech *does* have limits, as it should, but merely causing offence to someone else's strongly held political beliefs isn't such a limit. Nor should it be.

The Skelton Afternoon Tea Wars

A good example of the lockdown madness that seemed to engulf South Tees Conservatives, and much of the rest of the population at times, was the falling out among some of our Councillors in East Cleveland. Or the 'Wild East' as I came to call it.

The reason? The apparently divisive issue of afternoon teas.

One of our councillors ran a well regarded local cafe and caterers from premises on Skelton Industrial estate, an area of light industrial units presumably set up to help soften the loss of the last ironstone mine in the area in the 1960s. The premises looked suitably industrial on the outside but were welcoming and cosy on the inside.

The business provided popular sunday lunches, breakfasts, sandwiches and light snacks for local workers and residents alike. It was in many ways a social enterprise and had come into its own in helping out vulnerable local people with food parcels and meal deliveries in the early chaotic and worrying days of the first covid lockdown in March 2020. In fairness to all our local councillors in Skelton they all mucked in and helped out in covid relief efforts and I as local chairman made sure they were appreciated and knew it.

As living under covid restrictions became more 'normal' local businesses continued to adapt and re-invent what they did and how they did it. As people were now barred from going to cafes to eat out, various cafes in the area provided home delivery services, including that special treat of an afternoon tea of light sandwiches and cream cakes.

This seemingly innocuous and delightful practice gave rise to serious friction among our councillors when one of them made the mistake of posting on facebook, praising the afternoon tea available from a local business. This was based at a local former watermill; an antiques, afternoon tea and glamping concern, now diversifying into home delivered food to stay afloat during lockdown.

This proved to be like a red rag to a bull with the staff at the business of our other councillor, who took to sniping in replies to the post, casting aspersions about the freshness and quality of the offering from their rival.

And all hell broke loose. Seemingly the whole social media community in the Skeltons (there are at least four villages in close communion: Skelton itself, New Skelton, North Skelton, and Skelton Green) joined a pile on, on one side or another. Posters frantically bigging-up or slagging off the afternoon tea offerings from the rival businesses, or calling out how appalling it was that one business, especially one run by a local councillor, was apparently dissing a local rival who was also struggling to stay afloat in a pandemic.

Our councillor who started the whole thing off with their posting in praise of the mill's afternoon tea offering, pleaded, or feigned, innocence in doing so, but had clearly rubbed his Conservative Party colleague up the wrong way in doing so. And probably knew it would.

Meanwhile the councillor who owned the other business frantically backtracked and explained that they had known nothing about their staff's replies questioning the rival's product, and apologised for what was simply over-enthusiasm in speaking up for their own much-loved and high quality product.

Slowly, the anger subsided, tempers mellowed and facebook posts petered out. We had avoided a volley of rock cakes hurtling between cream-tea barricades on Skelton High Street.

Long-term, there seemed to be almost constant feuding between three of our Skelton councillors (two of whom were brothers!) Our senior councillor in the area, Cliff Foggo, the former RAF pilot and sometime rival for the Chairmanship of STCA, sensibly stayed out of it all and limited his social media posts to warnings about forthcoming road closures.

After the first lockdown ended one of our Skelton councillors, the cafe owner, defected to the independents on Redcar and Cleveland Council. Although her stated reason was discontent at the dull and uncommunicative leadership of Tory Group Leader Philip Thompson (and quite possibly a failed coup attempt against him) I can't help thinking that, shall we say, the sour taste left by the afternoon teas also played a part in it.

Burger Wars!

A slightly less sweet, but more meaty, conflict occurred somewhat later in the pandemic years among our Skelton councillors concerning control of a lucrative burger van pitch on another local industrial estate. Glasgow may have had its ice cream wars in the 1970s, and murderously violent they were too, but East Cleveland had a bit of a burger ding-dong, thankfully where the only blood spilled was bovine.

My namesake, Cllr Lee Holmes (no relation), was flipping burgers to earn some extra money and either his brother Craig, or our other local Tory councillor Craig (Julie) confusingly, had a rival interest in placing a burger van to feed the local grease monkeys, window fitters and gas engineers who inhabit such rural industrial estates. I lost track of who was rowing with who at various times but fraternal love, both political and familial, was often in short supply.

At one point a heated post by one councillor appeared on facebook making very serious allegations about one of the others, and I dreaded the thought that the minced beef was about to hit the fan again.

Fortunately, it disappeared as quickly as it appeared, so much so that I didn't even have time to take a screenshot for party records, or future memoirs, and fraternal peace appeared to be restored.

Blood is thicker than water, they say, but clearly in East Cleveland Conservative politics, burger grease is thickest of all.

"Kindly Go F#*k Yourself"

The fact that I share a name (not quite identical but near enough, for I am Lee Robert Holmes, he is Lee Brian Holmes) with a notorious local Conservative councillor caused much confusion, and some consternation, down the years of my involvement with South Tees Conservatives.

The fact 't'other Lee' as I came to call him had a, shall we say, colourful social media history only added to the amusement.

When I stood in a by-election in the neighbouring council area of Middlesbrough in 2021, even there there were local voters who thought I was the notorious Lee Holmes of 'black lives matter' and 'fag' shoes facebook controversy, and despite lots of explanation that I was in fact a completely different person, I'm not convinced I persuaded all those I came across of this strange quirk in Tory naming.

A minor further indiscretion the two Lees managed to keep out of the local press concerned a facebook exchange with a Labour supporter in Whitby. In what started out as an exchange about some local matter but then morphed into criticism of government welfare policy, the bedroom tax and such like, my namesake responded to a request that he 'kindly' comment on Tory policy with the bon-mot suggestion that "Perhaps you'd like to *kindly* go and fuck yourself"

This led to a complaint coming in by email to the local association and was passed to me as Chairman to deal with.

After a bit of snooping around on facebook I tracked down the offending exchange and noticed that the complainant had initially responded to the "fuck yourself" reply with a laughing face emoji.

Well, there you are, the power of the emoji.

You can hardly hold yourself out as mortally offended by a comment when your first response was to laugh along with it.

I replied to the complaint as professionally as possible, first explaining the strange fact that the subject of the complaint wasn't actually responding to it, and that I was in fact a completely different Lee Holmes to the councillor. And also no relation. So far, so good: no conflict of interest.

I then explained that the offending reply was clearly intended in good humour by Councillor Lee Holmes and had seemingly been received as such by the complainant, given the laughing emoji he responded with. Nonetheless I acknowledged that humour can be a dangerous thing (yet again) and that use of such language by a sitting councillor could look unprofessional. I said that I would discuss the exchange with the councillor, raise such concerns and no doubt he would learn from the experience.

I'm not sure if the complainant even bought the explanation that there were two Lee Holmes at South Tees, or the resolution to the complaint for that matter, but there were no further replies or repercussions for this Lee or t'other.

Chapter 16 - 'Dark Associations' - The Future

I'm hoping that you're enjoying this book and the (even if I say so myself) clever wordplay around its title 'Dark Associations'.

It's an entirely apt double-meaning incorporating the local party 'associations' that form the roots of the Tory tree, and in many ways it's lifeblood (or sap to keep the analogy going) and the dark happenings, attitudes and connections within, that give rise to the troubling stories I am recounting.

But there is also a further meaning behind the phrase that I want to address in this chapter: that those self-same associations may become literally 'dark', as ageing memberships, vitriolic splits, the party's unpopularity with voters and CCHQ's obsession for centralisation, threaten to permanently turn out the lights in associations right across the country.

Whether this would be a good or bad thing is perhaps open to question. I had wondered, both in my time as Chairman at South

Tees, and latterly while writing this book, whether ALL Conservative associations around the country were AS troubled as my own.

I've concluded, thankfully, that they are not. That South Tees is an extreme example that seems to exhibit *all* the worst qualities of the Conservative Party in one condensed, but accurate, study of the modern party.

I'm sure that other associations suffer similar scandals to our own, it would be odd if that were not the case, but I have yet to come across another that has experienced anywhere near the number and seriousness of those issues I dealt with at South Tees.

So, whilst I have perhaps had a particularly extreme baptism of fire into the nature of the modern Conservative Party, that experience is not invalidated by the unusual intensity of it. The party nationally is very much as I describe, and of course, the party centrally, at CCHQ, is *exactly* as I have experienced in this book. That is to say corrupt, inept and self-serving in equal measure.

In researching the wider context of this book, I have spoken to other former Chairmen and women in other associations and whilst they have recounted a variety of troubles: personality clashes, underhand behaviour, breaking of party rules, double-dealing and the malign hand of CCHQ in their experiences, none came close to the intensity or seriousness of the troubles at South Tees.

Far too often local associations are viewed by CCHQ and the party nationally as cannon fodder during elections and a cash cow to be milked regularly for the rest of the time. The number of recent elections and decline in high worth donors, especially in The City after Boris's 'F*#k business' mantra, led the party nationally to be so much on its uppers that they requested (required) every association in the country to donate a percentage of their own reserves to CCHQ during my tenure as Chairman. I suspect this request won't be the last.

Another common complaint I came across was the underhand way in which CCHQ seeks to impose its will on the associations around the country. This is especially so in the drive for centralisation and rationalisation in the party. CCHQ views the disparate and numerous small associations, especially in areas of the country such as the North East, as inefficient and ripe for a dose of the 'economies of scale' brought about by combining multiple associations into federations such as South Tees.

There are some merits to this, though as associations federate and become more distant from their local memberships it's suggested by older hands than me that both member numbers and engagement tend to decline. This was certainly the case when STCA was federated, and is likely to exacerbate declining membership caused by the party's current unpopularity and that dreadful term 'natural wastage', in an increasingly elderly party.

For despite my septuagenarian predecessor's assertion that the party's membership was not old, with an average age in the fifties, the Conservative Party IS an ageing party. Its membership is overwhelmingly either retired or in middle-age, with very few youngsters, other than the archetypal 'Tory Boy' clones attracted to join it. Indeed, why would young people be attracted to a party that has literally no 'offer' for them? Other than to work longer, and pay more taxes, to support the wealthier older generations who vote for the Tory party.

Part of this ongoing drive for centralisation included the 'North East Campaign Team' plan detailed elsewhere. Which interestingly seems to have died a death in the face of opposition from those with a real knowledge of the area and of how campaigning is best done in the modern era.

Another facet of CCHQ's centralisation mania was the grandly named 'Project Aduno' which was being developed in my final year at South Tees. This was an accounting package which would eventually be forced upon all associations (with a monthly fee payable to CCHQ for the privilege) that was designed to bring all reporting requirements, both financial and electoral, under one software system.

South Tees initially signed up for the pilot of this scheme, on the basis it was coming anyway and doing so would give us a couple of years use fee-free (careful with money as ever.) However, our involvement in even the pilot was continuously put back by the team at CCHQ.

I suspect this was due to glitches and faults in the software coming to light and one can't help feeling that given CCHQ's endemic ineptitude the end result was likely to be somewhat like the Post Office Horizon scandal. We may well have dodged a bullet by not being involved. It wouldn't have been beyond the realm of possibility to see local association officers up before the beak due to phantom financial shortfalls, rather like those many unfortunate Sub Postmasters and Mistresses.

When I last spoke to someone actively involved in the party, 'Project Aduno' meant nothing to them and it appears to have sunk without trace.

It's clear however that the drive for federation is still very much on, giving as it does, the party's centre at CCHQ greater control over a smaller number of associations and association officers. One of my contacts in the party regionally gave recent examples of how the 'right people' were being helped into association officer roles to ease this process along.

The danger for the party, among many others, is that alienating an already dwindling membership is likely to speed up the decline of the party in the country. If one were an optimist one might conclude that CCHQ had seen the danger of a declining membership and that centralisation was its favoured method to deal with it. But in my experience CCHQ isn't as far sighted as that, and this is really more an exercise in control freakery that will likely accelerate the decline of the Conservative Party as a mass movement party.

Politics and campaigning is undoubtedly changing, and changing at pace, with much greater emphasis on technology, both in terms of social media messaging, and also the identification of likely and possible supporters through the interrogation of the data thrown up by such social media platforms as Facebook. There is some merit in switching to this kind of less labour-intensive campaigning in the face of dwindling numbers of association members and activists. But that approach is only likely to accelerate the decline of the traditional Conservative Associations that have *been* the Conservative Party for so long.

So it may well be that this toxic combination of an ageing and alienated membership, natural wastage, splits and defections to other parties, having no 'offer' to entice younger members and endless centralisation drives will be the cause of a terminal decline for the traditional Conservative Party.

The 'dark associations' I have been detailing in this book may become literally just that, as the lights go out permanently in clubs and association offices all across the land.

Chapter 17 - Conclusion - The Bitter End?

By early 2024 we find a Conservative Party still clinging desperately to power, but convulsed by personal vendettas, ideological divisions and the already manoeuvring leadership campaigns of party rivals. All this even before the widely expected electoral drubbing due to come in the next twelve months.

How did we get here? What is the point of the party? Where do we likely go from here? And is the great survivor of British politics, the Conservative and Unionist Party of Great Britain and Northern Ireland really about to suffer a 1990s Canada style wipeout?

My experience of the Conservative Party, as a member, activist, local association chairman, and latterly critic, suggests that the dysfunction and poison in the current party may well be terminal. The rot in the Tory tree has well and truly set in, and it runs from the party's roots to its core.

Ironically, at this stage the party most reminds me of the old Communist Party of the Soviet Union circa 1991. Obviously not in terms of its political ideology, but rather its cynical, self-serving corruption and desire to cling to power whatever the cost. Like the old Communist Party, the Conservative Party has long since given up any attempt to govern in the national interest. In the Tories' case they have done so in favour of their own self-interest and of protecting the narrow interests of the super-wealthy donors who keep them afloat. Some of them, ironically, foreign oligarchs hailing from the former Soviet Union itself, who made their money in that country's chaotic collapse.

The dangers of this dependence on a small number of super-rich donors has most recently been dramatically illustrated by the racist bile spewed out by Frank Hester, the £15 million Tory donor. The initial reluctance of Number 10 and senior ministers to call out this grotesque racism is an indicator of just how valued such people are, and what influence they hold over the party. As is the reluctance of the party to hand any of the tainted dosh back.

My experience suggests that the only other interest the Conservative Party now serves is that of trying to ensure its own survival, and in that cause any sense of morality or common human decency has seemingly been discarded. It is a party that has lost whatever moral compass it ever had.

Examples of this are numerous:

Its mistreatment of Jade Smith, whose suicide was at least in part due to that mistreatment, was appalling. Its public promise of an investigation into her death, which never actually materialised, was just as bad. It also highlights the pure cynicism of a party willing to promise almost anything to cover its back in the short-term, without ever having any intent to honour that promise.

The apparent prior knowledge of serious sexual offences that Jade alleged, committed by a clearly unsuitable character who was nonetheless allowed to become a Conservative councillor, with all the risk that entails, also demonstrates that lack of a moral compass.

For the sake of short term political expediency the party is willing to take on board members and candidates who in previous times would have been regarded as person non grata. David Smith was perhaps a grotesquely extreme example of that, but nationally the party has also shown itself willing to welcome onboard, and promote, figures who are not really Conservatives at all, and who jump ship (with great embarrassment to the party) at the earliest opportunity. Such characters abound but most recently and newsworthily, I might of course be referring to former Deputy Party Chairman Lee Anderson.

In addition, the Smith case, that of Imran Ahmed Khan, and the local candidate later found to be a drunken racist thug, displays a lack of proper vetting, and the desperation of a party short of supporters, but trying perhaps too hard to capitalise on the short term popularity brought by Brexit. The current, very long list, of Tory MPs suspended or expelled for a variety of misbehaviours, the most recent being Mark Menzies of 'bad people' fame, suggests an even deeper malaise in party culture, selections and promotions. Why does the Conservative party attract, and promote, so many sociopaths?

This desperation to capitalise on a sudden, new found popularity in local terms also finds a much broader parallel in the party's desire to pander to new, and less traditionally 'Conservative' supporters nationally. In selling its soul to accommodate individuals and opinions more at home on the far-right, the party has bought itself some short term political success, but at a cost that seems likely to tear it apart in the next few years. A large part of the mess the party finds itself in currently, with Rishi Sunak having little apparent authority in an increasingly ungovernable party, stems from this chasing of support from dubious sources.

This tendency can be traced at least as far back as David Cameron's master plan to destroy the threat from Ukip by means of the EU referendum, which in fact only served to destroy Cameron himself and drastically change the nature of the Tory party through an influx of Ukippers. PCC Steve Turner being a prime example locally.

The party's failure to investigate the circumstances behind David Smith's selection as a council candidate, including the alleged prior knowledge of offending highlighted by Jade herself, again emphasises that self-preservation and cover-ups trump morality in all the party now does.

That the party has clearly learned nothing from the tragic death of Jade Smith, and the role its treatment played in that, is clear from its later treatment of bullying allegations in the local office of one of its MPs, and the whistleblower who threatened to make those allegations public. Rather than take on board and deal with those complaints, the fact the party, and those in it, thought it was appropriate to make a criminal allegation of blackmail against that volunteer (who was also a long standing friend of the MP and his hardest working volunteer) speaks volumes of the party's debased view of morality in the present day.

The fact the party knew that individual to be vulnerable and went ahead with that police complaint anyway, in full knowledge of Jade Smith's suicide, another vulnerable local activist, adds an extra level of corrupted morality.

All normal considerations of gratitude, loyalty, common human decency or simple concern for human wellbeing were subsumed by the overwhelming need to do whatever is necessary to cover the party's back. To protect its reputation. To ensure its survival.

These cases illustrate that, like the old Soviet Communist Party, the protection and preservation of the 'Party' is now all that matters. All other considerations are irrelevant.

The party's failure to acknowledge those allegations, let alone answer them, adds an extra layer of Orwellian immorality and newspeak to the story of the current Conservative Party.

From the local MP to the party nationally and even the leadership of the voluntary party, in National Convention Chairman, Peter Booth, there has been an unwillingness to face up to these serious issues. This head-in-the-sand approach adds the other crucial element of incompetence to the party's current character. There is perhaps no worse combination than corruption *and* ineptitude, and in my experience it's a combination the party currently suffers from in spades.

Of course the party talks a good game on safeguarding and protecting the rights of party workers and volunteers. But in my experience, talk is all it is. Talk to improve the image of the party, talk to reassure volunteers, and when necessary, talk to cover the party's back. But of action there is little, and when action actually occurs it is taken purely to, yet again, protect the party's image. To cover the party's back.

Which all begs the question of how the party has come to this state in its evolution?

To my mind there are a number of causes behind this corruption, behind this rot in the Tory tree.

First and foremost the culture of the Conservative Party is at fault. It is a party that seems to attract some of the most unsuitable individuals, both among its candidates and its paid 'professional' staff.

Too many at CCHQ and in the party organisation seem to regard politics as a sport: a game to be played purely to get one over on your opponents, be they in the party or outside it, rather than as an exercise in public service or good government. Just as big business apparently attracts a high proportion of psychopaths, according to various psychological studies, I get the sense that so does the Conservative Party. And given the culture therein they tend to thrive and rise within it: one only has to look at the number of Tory MPs having faced serious allegations of criminal or financial misconduct for evidence of this. I'm non-partisan enough to see that this is a problem across all political parties, misbehaviour is not a Tory-only trait, but it seems to have a particular hold in the Conservative Party, in my experience.

The danger for the country in this is not just the development of a cynical and divisive political culture that seeks political advantage at any cost to social cohesion and civil society, but in the short-termism that clearly afflicts the UK. Why go for long-term necessary reforms that may prove unpopular in the short term, if your only view of politics is that it's a game to be played for instant political advantage?

Theresa May's brave attempt to find a solution to funding adult social care at the 2017 general election was perhaps the only example of a longer-term attempt to solve a pressing social problem I can recall. But its disastrous fate, and mauling by those imbued with the prevailing cynical culture in politics, is illustrative of the problem we face in politics generally and in the Conservative Party in particular.

Whilst the party, and politics more widely, is largely populated at all levels by career politicians with little experience or even interest outside politics, this cynical view of politics as a game is only going to continue. And the governance of the United Kingdom will continue to suffer.

As for the Conservative Party itself, its own membership is sadly another reason for its decline and quite possible extinction.

The party membership IS elderly, and this is hardly surprising when the party has so little to offer the young, and as this tale illustrates all too often mistreats its own members.

The age of the party membership obviously offers practical problems in terms of campaigning, though in fairness I have come across many dedicated older activists who can leaflet and canvass with the best of them. But in reality older legs and eyes and hearts can only do so much and unless the party finds some way of appealing to a younger demographic, the decline in activism may prove terminal.

This problem is also reflected in fewer and fewer party members being willing to take on the roles of party officials in local associations and federations such as STCA. My own experience proves it to be a thankless and demanding task that offers few rewards at some not inconsiderable personal risk, be it legal, reputational or psychological. I hope I got out in time and am still on the right side of crazy. I'll let you decide.

The party's answer to this problem of more federation, fewer local associations and more and more control from an often inept centre risks creating a death spiral of disinterest and disconnection among the members that remain.

The membership has also clearly been problematic in terms of leadership selection, most glaringly with the Liz Truss debacle.

Whilst the choice, and adoration, of Boris Johnson as party leader was perhaps understandable given the state of the party and country in early 2019 (a choice I myself made) the weird nostalgia and unrealistic political dogma that led to the choice of Liz Truss by the party membership in 2022, was extraordinary, and points to a deeper cultural problem among party members. One that if repeated risks driving the party even further into a far-right wilderness after the next election that it may struggle to return from. The Corbynite 'Long March' in the Labour Party after 2015 may well find its mirror image in the Conservative Party post 2024, and given the current state of the party may prove terminal.

There is no easy solution to this problem, and merely removing the right to elect party leaders from the membership is problematic in itself. The sense that Rishi Sunak is lacking in legitimacy, as not being chosen by members, is widely held by members, especially on the ukippy right of the party. This undoubtedly contributes to the current instability in the party. Among many, many other factors.

The influx of former Ukippers to the party post 2016, and the exodus or expulsion of pro EU Remainers, has also radically changed the ethos and outlook of the party. And not for the better (and I say that as a Leave voter myself) The traditional, pragmatic, pro-business, sound-money, small-but-effective government Conservatives of old have morphed into a far more dogmatic, unrealistic and right-wing party that would seemingly rather have doctrinal purity rather than power. Or competence, for that matter.

If I'm painting a bleak picture of the Conservative Party's present and potential future, it's one borne of experience within the party itself and of politics more generally, as the political nerd that I am. The present and past are done and a closed book (as soon will this be) but the future is, of course, yet to be determined.

My political nerdery does remind me that the Conservative Party is the great survivor not just in British democracy, but in world democracy, and it may be premature, not to say reckless, to begin writing its obituary right now. But its faults, problems and internal contradictions are now so numerous that the 'broad church' that it once represented on the centre-right of British politics is looking dangerously derelict.

If this book serves as even a minor sledgehammer to add to its demolition then it will have served its purpose. For the people of Britain deserve something better than the current Conservative Party, and if it takes complete demolition and a rebuild to bring that about, then let the wrecking ball swing.

Epilogue - Mugged Off

I've covered my more venal motives for writing this book in the chapter on motive at the front. Whilst never donning silky whiskers and a luxuriant tail (not publicly at least) I have revealed myself to be a member of the cat-tendency when it comes to reacting to ill-treatment. Revenge IS a dish best served cold, and preferably with a side helping of tuna.

I do also have less personal and base reasons for writing this book, of course: revulsion at the corruption, immorality, illegality and cover-ups I have experienced in the party, as well as a general sense of horror at just how incompetent, extreme and unpleasant the Conservative Party has become in recent years, and these are detailed throughout the book. I hope readers will have regard to these more noble reasons as well as my more petty personal grievances when assessing my motives.

Though I *do* feel ill-treated by the Conservative Party, albeit far less so than many of its real victims that I've detailed elsewhere in this book.

In particular, my application to become a prospective parliamentary candidate for the party was thrown out at the first hurdle, despite the years of hard work promoting the party and clearing up its numerous messes at South Tees. For, to paraphrase the role of 'The Hand' in Game of Thrones, the party shits and the Chairman cleans it up.

This rejection came at the criminal references and suitability check, which was particularly insulting and alarming given how actual rogues like PCC Steve Turner have prospered in the party. The worse you are, the better you seem to do in the current, deeply corrupt Tory party.

For I definitely have no criminal record, not even police cautions, and only one speeding ticket from many years ago on the M180 in South Humberside. Which at the time was very quiet, as I believe it was being re-cobbled.

The 'offence' that got me 'mugged off' by the party's Candidates Team, despite years of hard work for the Tories, was to be honest and plain speaking in a party that now values neither quality. I'm not sure if hailing from Yorkshire, where such honesty is still valued, counts as a protected ethnic identity that would ground a claim for discrimination, but I suspect not.

After fighting to get a reason for my rejection (which are never normally disclosed), motivated in particular by the thought that it was a character check that I had failed on, I finally found out that *two* offending tweets had been uncovered, which the party found unacceptable and grounds for rejection. So I at least had the satisfaction of knowing that my (largely) blame-free life devoid of criminality hadn't actually been *held against me.*

The nature of these offending tweets do raise interesting questions about the Conservative Party's much lauded commitment to free speech and freedom of thought. Which as it turns out proves to be as illusory and false as most other things in the current Conservative Party.

The first tweet, dated from before my active involvement in the party, though I believe I was a member at the time, was a throw away comment in response to somebody on twitter accusing me of being a Boris fanboy. In reply, I said that actually I felt that Johnson was a 'buffoon' (which he is.)

This was around the time that Johnson was making an ass of himself out of government, having resigned as Foreign Secretary over May's Brexit deal, where he had previously been making an ass of himself. About the time of well-paid newspaper columns decrying muslim women as looking like 'pillar boxes' and 'bank robbers, or describing money spent investigating historic sexual abuse (Jimmy Savile and the like) as being 'spaffed up the wall.' So far, so buffoonish. Offensive even.

I am a political realist however, and given that Johnson had miraculously by then (including getting my support) become Tory leader and PM, I realise that such a tweet would have been difficult for a parliamentary candidate to explain or defend, if it came to light. As they do tend to do in this dangerous age.

As self censorship can be a good thing, and given I had actually voted for Boris to become leader, I would have happily deleted the tweet, not least as it was no longer an accurate reflection of my opinion. Which was now that Johnson was merely buffoonish, rather than a buffoon, perhaps?

Sadly, I was never given the opportunity to explain my opinion or delete the tweet, but simply mugged off with a rejection email without further explanation, until I demanded it.

The second tweet that was regarded as offensive or unacceptable, was *ironically* a tweet defending Boris Johnson's right to ask searching questions about Islam in his book 'The Dream of Rome.' Johnson IS a classical scholar, and whilst his works have a populist flavour, he is entitled to ask historical questions about the impact of Islam on the post Roman world, as his book did. It's a legitimate line of historic enquiry, or should be in any free society.

Specifically, it made the argument, that following Islam's initial great flourishing in the arts, culture, and science, that Islam had actually hampered human development in the muslim world. It's a controversial argument, but one that in a free society, an author should be free to make, just as others should be free to criticise and rebut with counter-arguments.

My tweet (in response to a discussion on Channel Five current affairs show 'Jeremy Vine') was as follows:

So the politically correct think you must not critically examine the historical impact of Islam on human development? Does this apply to all religions? #darkdays #JeremyVine

I made this point as someone who believes in academic freedom and more broadly in freedom of thought and of religion. Crucially, I also made it as a secular humanist (who rather dislikes all organised religion) rather than somebody with a particular beef about Islam.

But apparently, in the modern Conservative Party, that makes such a furore about defending freedom of speech and thought, and opposing 'cancel culture', that tweet was verboten and, ironically enough, saw me cancelled.

Given what had happened to my predecessor as Chairman perhaps I should have been more careful on discussing Islam at all, but my opinions were nothing like the openly islamophobic views expressed in that earlier case. And freedom of speech, even on controversial issues, is something we neglect at our peril.

As I sat somewhat nonplussed in the Teams meeting the Candidates Team had arranged to address my concerns (thankfully they decided against dragging me down to their office in Leeds, which would have added insult to injury) I said that if being a candidate would impose such restrictions on making such innocuous statements, I'm not sure I would want to be a candidate in the first place.

In fairness to the head of the Candidates Team in the meeting, who appeared to nod sagely in agreement with me, it seems that I was not alone in viewing rejection on such freedom of speech issues as deeply unfair and troubling. Yet the rejection stood.

It is perhaps no wonder that the party now has so many inadequate MPs in its ranks, Yes Men, and identikit politicians unwilling to ask difficult questions, plus the numerous revealed sociopaths, when freedom of thought and honesty is regarded as forbidden, but checks on genuine moral and criminal suitability are clearly inadequate.

For the parliamentary party has had so many scandals in recent years, and has produced so little actual talent, that party selection processes are failing to weed out the wrong-uns, whilst mugging off decent candidates who happen to favour openness, honesty and plain speaking. Even if I say so myself. Which I do.

With hindsight, given all that has happened in the Conservative Party, both locally and nationally, since that day in 2022, I have to say that I'm now grateful for the Candidate Team's rejection of my application.

It freed me from the need to try to defend the absolute shambles that the Conservative Party and government have become in the meantime, be it Johnson's constant lying, Truss' catastrophic cosplay as PM, or Sunak's weakness in controlling the more extreme far-right elements now clearly present in the party.

It also saved me from getting my sorry ass handed to me by an electorate clearly now utterly done with the Tory party.

It has also freed me to write this book, detailing the abuses in the party that I have witnessed, and in doing so hopefully either contributing to its imminent destruction, or at the least pointing it in the direction of much needed reform.

And at the very, very least it has also satisfied my rather primal need for revenge.

Miaow.